# Atlantis Illustrated

# Atlantis Illustrated

## H.R. STAHEL

FOREWORD BY
**ISAAC ASIMOV**

Grosset & Dunlap
Publishers ● New York

Excerpts reprinted from Plato's *Timaeus & Critias*, trans. by H.D.P. Lee,
   Penguin Classics, Revised Edition, 1971
Copyright © 1965, 1971 by H.D.P. Lee
Reprinted by permission of Penguin Books Ltd

Foreword Copyright © 1982 by Isaac Asimov

For my daughters
Barbara and Annina

# Contents

Foreword 1

Introduction 3

Prologue 7

The Empire 9

The Island 15

Poseidon's Rings 19

The Canal Network 23

Rural Atlantis 31

The Building of the Palace 35

The Construction of the Bridges 41

The Subterranean Channels and Docks 51

The Temple of Poseidon 61

The Completed Acropolis 67

The Completed Ring Islands 71

The Canal to the Sea 81

The Walls and the Towers 93

Atlantis in Cross Section 106

Epilogue 119

# Foreword by Isaac Asimov

About 1500 B.C. the small island of Thera in the Aegean Sea, a hundred miles north of Crete, blew up in a tremendous explosion.

The whole island was a volcano that had suddenly come to devastating life. An advanced and civilized place, it was utterly destroyed in the explosion, and every person upon it was killed. The sea still rolls over its pulverized center and only the broken rim of the island still exists.

The explosion permanently weakened the flourishing civilization on the large island of Crete, and set up tidal waves that washed destruction over the shores of Greece and Asia Minor.

For over a thousand years the tale of that immense catastrophe lived on in the minds of the people of the eastern Mediterranean. When, about 380 B.C., the Greek philosopher Plato wished to tell a story of how a great civilization came to be destroyed, he told the tale of Thera.

However, the tale was expanded. The Aegean Sea seemed too small an arena for such a cataclysm in a day when the horizons of geography had expanded far beyond the limits of ancient Cretan times. Plato therefore imagined the exploding island to have been far larger, far more powerful, and far more magnificent than Thera had been. And he placed it beyond the Pillars of Hercules, in the vague mists of the unknown Atlantic Ocean, where magnificence has room to spread itself.

He invented the tale of Atlantis.

Atlantis totally captured the minds of Western humanity. No imaginary place has ever been more famous. In fact, uncounted people have taken Plato's fable for truth and have imagined that Atlantis really existed thousands of years ago in mid-Atlantic. Those who did not believe Plato had it quite right tried to find traces of some distant civilization that might have served as the kernel of truth behind the story. The actual tale of Thera, the real basis, was not known until excavations, begun as recently as 1966, uncovered it.

And yet, true or not, the tale of Atlantis is magic, and it was conceived by one of the great minds of all times. We have every right to ask: What was Atlantis like *in the mind of Plato*?

Atlantis may not have really existed, but it has, after all, affected every generation in the last twenty-three centuries just as though it *had* existed. Why, then, shouldn't we want to know what it looks like? Mr. H. R. Stahel brings an architect's expertise to the task of rebuilding Atlantis on the basis of Plato's exact words, and produces before our eyes the very land that has lived more brightly and beautifully in fantasy than almost any other has in reality.

See for yourself.

# Introduction

The story of Atlantis, which so captured the Western imagination, first appears in literature in two later dialogues of Plato, written about 2,300 years ago. The mention in the *Timaeus* is fairly brief, as Plato merely uses the ancient war between Athens and Atlantis as a starting point for a consideration of the workings of the ideal state. In the *Critias*, however, Atlantis is fully and physically described—and what a fascinating world it must have been.

Plato's text is only twenty or so pages long, and even this material is incomplete, ending as it does in midsentence. Yet over the centuries it has inspired some 25,000 books, in all languages; the earliest was written in 200 B.C., the most recent is probably in preparation somewhere today.

But although an incredibly large amount has been written about Atlantis, there are very few illustrations or drawings, and most of these are maps that reveal varying degrees of inexactitude. On the whole the artists were apparently satisfied to depict the circular bands of water with an overdimensional mountain in the background. Such renderings are all the more lamentable when one considers how precisely Plato described this remarkable place.

This is the aspect of the Atlantis story that fascinated me, not speculation about its origin or end, not philosophical inquiry into the nature of utopia. But working from Plato's descriptions—and ultimately we have no other—I wanted to answer in plans and drawings the simple question, *what did it look like?*

3

The text is no formal blueprint. The chronology, intermingling the history and works of gods and men, is uncertain; the name "Atlantis" can mean the empire, the island, or the capital city; useful pieces of description are sometimes scattered through the text and need to be brought together for the picture to emerge (hence the connecting ellipses in some of the quotations from the *Critias*). Still, it is in the words of Plato that are found the measurements and specifications that permit reconstruction. In some instances, his descriptions are more detailed than in others, and while the plans are all to scale, the drawings are not. But I believe that in no regard are these illustrations inconsistent with the Atlantis of the dialogues.

The words of Homer led the great Schliemann to find Troy in Asia Minor. Similarly, Plato's words will enable us to find Atlantis in the mind's eye.

# Atlantis Illustrated

μακροῦ δὲ δὴ λόγου τοιάδε τις ἦν ἀρχή τότε. καθάπερ
ἐν τοῖς πρόσθεν ἐλέχθη περὶ τῆς τῶν θεῶν λήξεως,
ὅτι κατενείμαντο γῆν πᾶσαν ἔνθα μὲν μείζους
λήξεις, ἔνθα δὲ καὶ ἐλάττους, ἱερὰ θυσίας τε αὑτοῖς
κατασκευάζοντες, οὕτω δὴ καὶ τὴν νῆσον Ποσειδῶν
τὴν Ἀτλαντίδα λαχὼν ἐκγόνους αὑτοῦ κατῴκισεν
ἐκ θνητῆς γυναικὸς γεννήσας ἔν τινι τόπῳ τοιῷδε
τῆς νήσου.... παίδων δὲ ἀρρένων πέντε γενέσεις
διδύμους γεννησάμενος ἐθρέψατο, καὶ τὴν νῆσον
τὴν Ἀτλαντίδα πᾶσαν δέκα μέρη κατανείμας
τῶν μὲν πρεσβυτάτων τῷ προτέρῳ γενομένῳ
τήν τε μητρῴαν οἴκησιν καὶ τὴν κύκλῳ λῆξιν,
πλείστην καὶ ἀρίστην οὖσαν, ἀπένειμε, βασιλέα
τε τῶν ἄλλων κατέστησε, τοὺς δὲ ἄλλους
ἄρχοντας, ἑκάστῳ δὲ ἀρχὴν πολλῶν ἀνθρώπων
καὶ τόπον πολλῆς χώρας ἔδωκεν. ὀνόματα δὲ
πᾶσιν ἔθετο, τῷ μὲν πρεσβυτάτῳ καὶ βασιλεῖ
τοῦτο οὗ δὴ καὶ πᾶσα ἡ νῆσος τό τε πέλαγος
ἔσχεν ἐπωνυμίαν, Ἀτλαντικὸν λεχθέν, ὅτι
τοὔνομ' ἦν τῷ πρώτῳ βασιλεύσαντι τότε Ἄτλας·
KPITIAΣ

6

# Prologue

*The story is a long one and it begins like this. We have already mentioned how the gods distributed the whole earth between them in larger or smaller shares and then established shrines and sacrifices for themselves. Poseidon's share was the island of Atlantis and he settled the children borne to him by a mortal woman in a particular district of it. . . . He begot five pairs of male twins, brought them up, and divided the island of Atlantis into ten parts which he distributed between them. He allotted the elder of the eldest pair of twins his mother's home district and the land surrounding it, the biggest and best allocation, and made him King over the others; the others he made governors, each of a populous and large territory. He gave them all names. The eldest, the King, he gave a name from which the whole island and surrounding ocean took their designation of 'Atlantic', deriving it from Atlas the first King.*

CRITIAS

# The Empire

*Our records tell how your city [Athens] checked a great power which arrogantly advanced from its base in the Atlantic ocean to attack the cities of Europe and Asia. For in those days the Atlantic was navigable. There was an island opposite the strait which you call (so you say) the Pillars of Heracles, an island larger than Libya and Asia combined; from it travellers could in those days reach the other islands, and from them the whole opposite continent which surrounds what can truly be called the ocean. For the sea within the strait we were talking about is like a lake with a narrow entrance; the outer ocean is the real ocean and the land which entirely surrounds it is properly termed continent. On this island of Atlantis had arisen a powerful and remarkable dynasty of kings, who ruled the whole island, and many other islands as well and parts of the continent; in addition it controlled, within the strait, Libya up to the borders of Egypt and Europe as far as Tyrrhenia.*

TIMAEUS

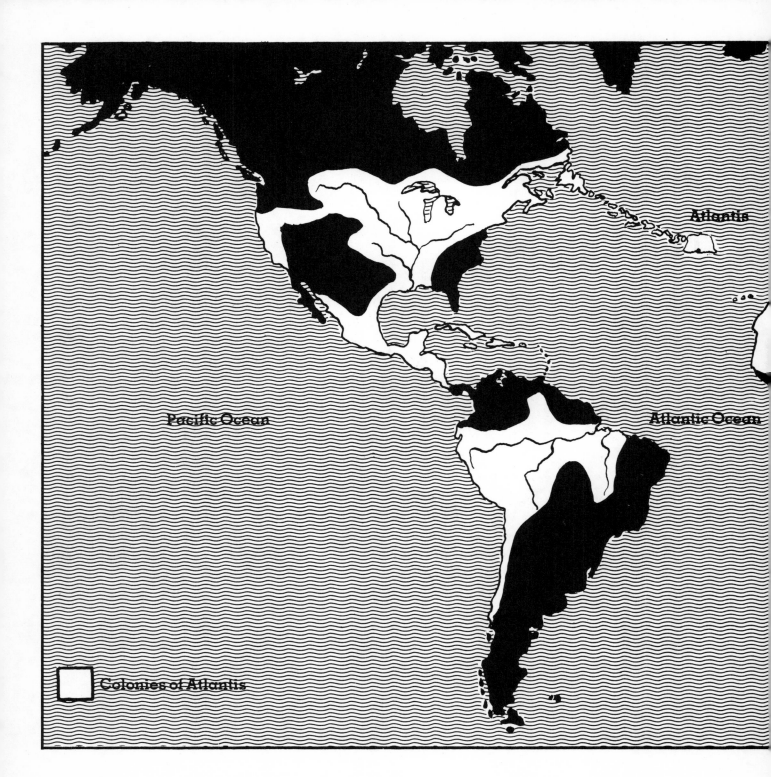

Atlantis

Pacific Ocean

Atlantic Ocean

Colonies of Atlantis

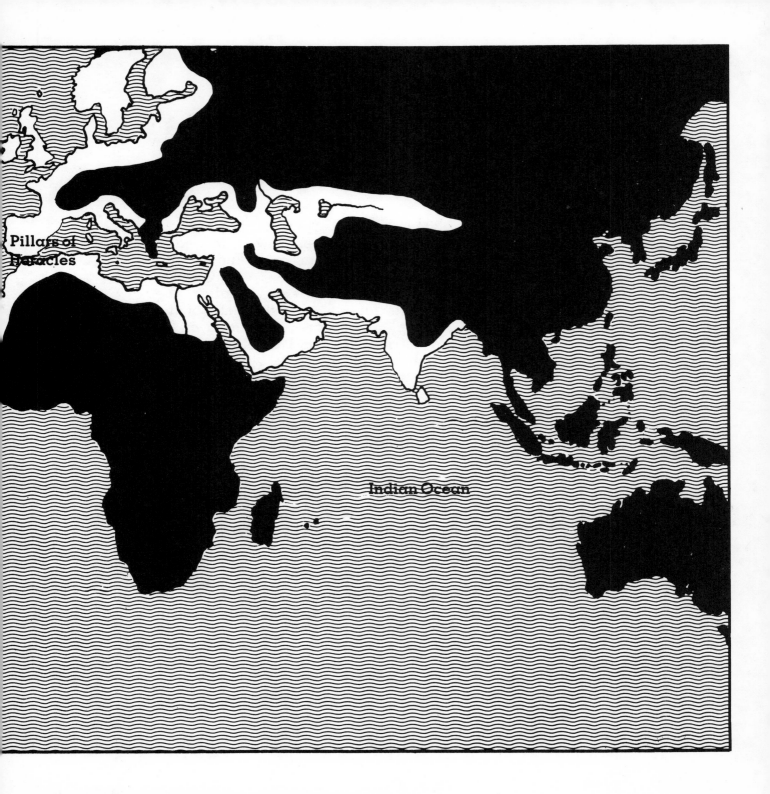

Pillars of Heracles

Indian Ocean

# THE EMPIRE OF ATLANTIS

Plato was writing 2,300 years ago of events that had occurred 9,000 years before his own time. Eleven thousand years ago, then, the Atlantic Ocean was well known and navigable; by his day, that was no longer true. To the Greeks, the Pillars of Heracles guarding the Strait of Gibraltar, the gateway to the western Mediterranean, was the limit of the world they bustled in. Plato clearly locates the island of Atlantis outside the Pillars of Heracles, and carefully distinguishes between the Mediterranean, the "lake with a narrow entrance" that was familiar to the seafaring Greeks, and the "real ocean," the Atlantic.

From the island travelers could reach other islands and then an entire continent; in other words, it was then possible to "island-hop" west from Atlantis to the shore of the North American continent.

At its height the empire of Atlantis extended over much of the known world. Atlantan colonies spread over the Americas, Europe (as far as Italy), and North Africa. Farther east, the empire had dominion over the Middle East, the shores of the Caspian Sea and the Black Sea, and much of the Indian subcontinent.

The revenues from these worldwide colonies were beyond measure, and it comes as no surprise that the royal city of Atlantis, the center of the empire, will be built in such splendid and monumental fashion.

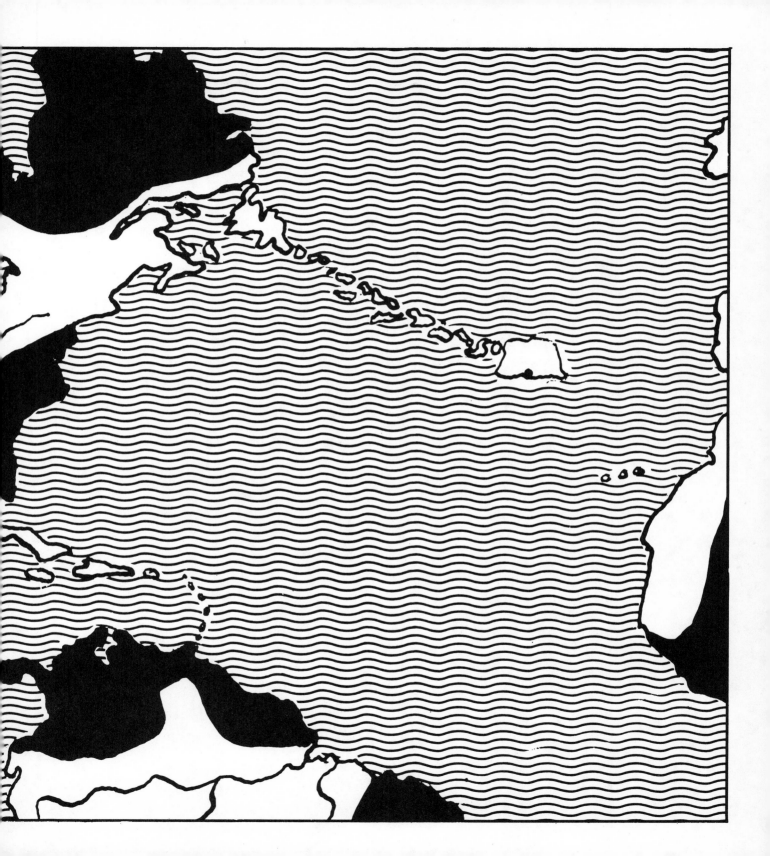

# The Island

*To begin with the region as a whole was said to be high above the level of the sea, from which it rose precipitously; the city was surrounded by a uniformly flat plain, which was in turn enclosed by mountains which came right down to the sea. This plain was rectangular in shape, measuring three thousand stades in length and at its midpoint two thousand stades in breadth from the coast. This whole area of the island faced south, and was sheltered from the north winds. The mountains which surrounded it were celebrated as being more numerous, higher and more beautiful than any which exist today; and in them were numerous villages and a wealthy population, as well as rivers and lakes and meadows, which provided ample pasture for all kinds of domesticated and wild animals, and a plentiful variety of woodland to supply abundant timber for every kind of manufacture.*

CRITIAS

The measurements Plato gives are in the Greek units of foot, plethron, and stade. Although we know from the measurements of different classical ruins that the standard for the length of the foot varied in historic Greece (most commonly ranging from .29 meter to .33 meter), the relationship of the three units was constant: 100 feet always equaled 1 plethron, 6 plethra always equaled 1 stade. Since the modern English foot at .3048 meter is within the range of the ancient Greek equivalents, the reader need make no further calculations. I have used 1 foot as equal to .30 meter; 1 stade, then, equals 180 meters.

Thus, the plain of Atlantis extended over an area of more than 77,000 square miles, the size and, roughly, the shape of the state of Nebraska. Forming a sort of horseshoe, hills and mountains were ranged along the East and West Coasts, gradually rising toward the north, with high mountain chains along the North Coast. Rivers, lakes, and swamps were scattered through the densely forested plain. Offshore to the west are shown the beginnings of a chain of islands forming the connection with North America.

In the drawing, to show its location I have exaggerated the size of the hill on the South Coast, where the Acropolis of Atlantis will be built.

N

THE ISLAND OF ATLANTIS

# Poseidon's Rings

*At the centre of the island,\* near the sea, was a plain, said to be the most beautiful and fertile of all plains, and near the middle of this plain about fifty stades inland a hill of no great size. Here there lived one of the original earth-born inhabitants called Evenor, with his wife Leucippe. They had an only child, a daughter called Cleito. She was just of marriageable age when her father and mother died, and Poseidon was attracted by her and had intercourse with her, and fortified the hill where she lived by enclosing it with concentric rings of sea and land. There were two rings of land and three of sea, like cartwheels, with the island at their centre and equidistant from each other, making the place inaccessible to man (for there were still no ships or sailing in those days). He equipped the central island with godlike lavishness; he made two springs flow, one of hot and one of cold water, and caused the earth to grow abundant produce of every kind.*

CRITIAS

---

\*The translator points out that this means "midway along its greatest length."

The first builder of Atlantis was the god Poseidon, who gave the city its famous and unique form when he dug three concentric moats to protect his home, thus creating the characteristic Ring Islands. The hill on which he and his wife, Cleito, lived (with, in time, their five sets of twins!) was about five and a half miles inland from the South Coast. In those days, no channels were yet cut nor bridges built—then truly the Central Island of Atlantis was "inaccessible to man."

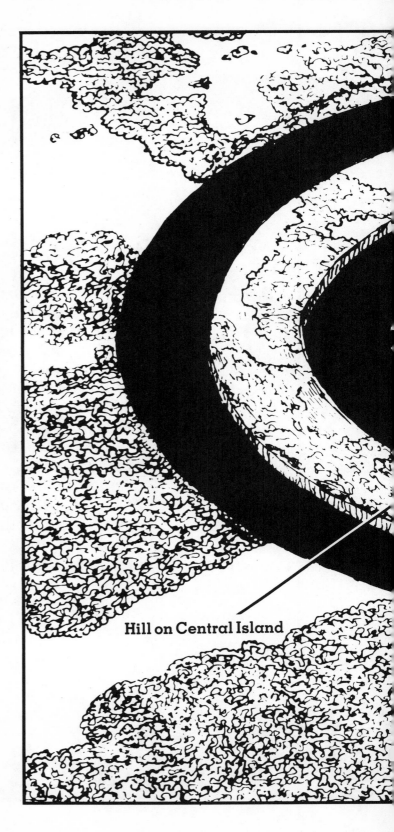

Hill on Central Island

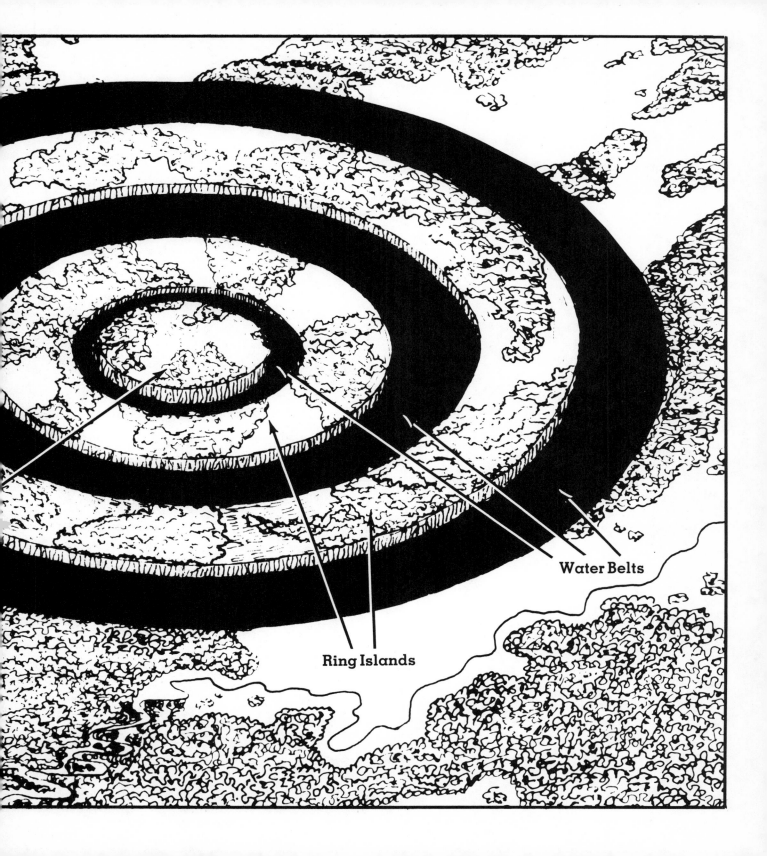

Water Belts

Ring Islands

# The Canal Network

*Over a long period of time the work of a number of kings had effected certain modifications in the natural features of the plain. It was naturally a long, regular rectangle; and any defects in its shape were corrected by means of a ditch dug round it. The depth and breadth and length of this may sound incredible for an artificial structure when compared with others of a similar kind, but I must give them as I heard them. The depth was a hundred feet, the width a stade, and the length, since it was dug right round the plain, was ten thousand stades. The rivers which flowed down from the mountains emptied into it, and it made a complete circuit of the plain, running round to the city from both directions, and there discharging into the sea. Channels about a hundred feet broad were cut from the ditch's landward limb straight across the plain, at a distance of a hundred stades from each other, till they ran into it on its seaward side. They cut cross channels between them and also to the city, and used the whole complex to float timber down from the mountains and transport seasonal produce by boat. They had two harvests a year, a winter one for which they relied on rainfall and a summer one for which the channels, fed by the rivers, provided irrigation.*

CRITIAS

When I began to reconstruct in plans and drawings the empire, the island, and the city of Atlantis, I started by making a plan of the vast shore plain surrounding the city. The great ditch, 100 feet deep and 600 feet across, that surrounded it was almost 1,200 miles long—no wonder Plato allows that the dimensions he gives may sound incredible!

Plato also gives the layout and measurements of the north-south channels from the mountains bordering the "landward limb" of the plain to the sea, and of the east-west cross channels. The grid these figures produce is schematic—the arithmetic does not allow for the width of the channels.

The extensive main and subsidiary canals that crisscrossed the plain totaled 14,000 miles. This figure does not include smaller irrigation canals for local distribution of water, nor the channels that supplied drinking water. The reference to two harvests a year, one of them depending on the canal network, is a strong suggestion that water was retained in the canals; the mention of transport by boat implies a system of dams and sluices. Plato himself could hardly believe in such a stupendous network—but he emphasizes that it had been accomplished by men, not gods.

Now, placing the grid on a drawing of the island:

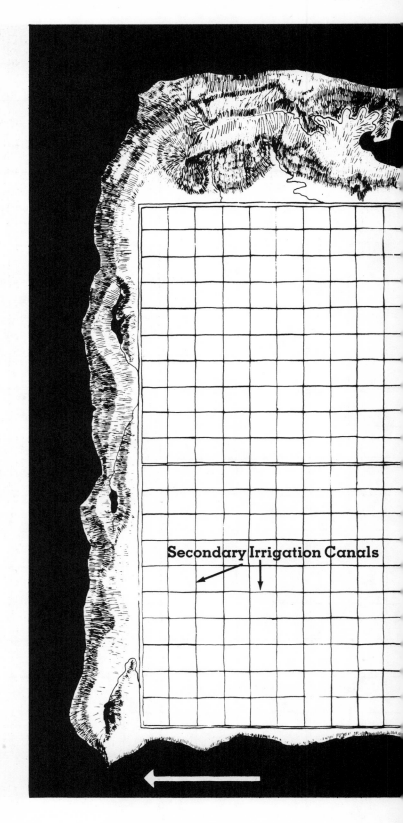

Secondary Irrigation Canals

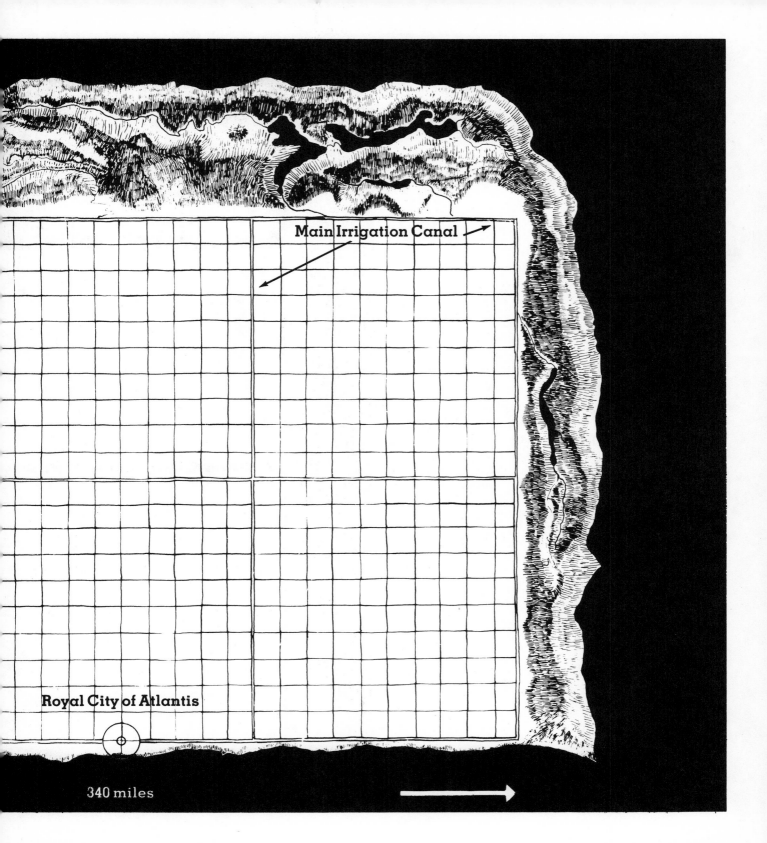

Main Irrigation Canal

Royal City of Atlantis

340 miles

And Atlantis itself? With the information we already have we can place the great ringed city in its true location on the plain. The dotted outline of Manhattan shows comparison of size.

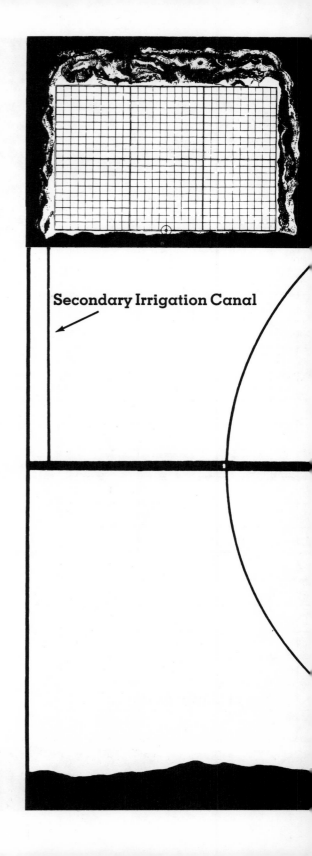

Secondary Irrigation Canal

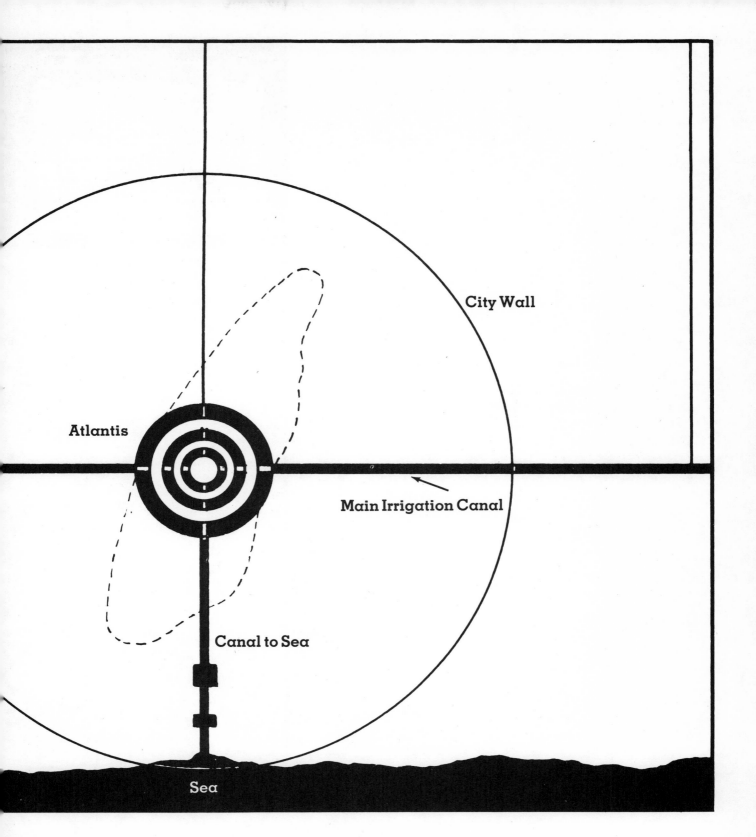

# Rural Atlantis

*Because of the extent of their power they received many imports, but for most of their needs the island itself provided. It had mineral resources from which were mined both solid materials and metals, including one metal which survives today only in name, but was then mined in quantities in a number of localities in the island, orichalc, in those days the most valuable metal except gold. There was a plentiful supply of timber for structural purposes, and every kind of animal domesticated and wild, among them numerous elephants. For there was plenty of grazing for this largest and most voracious of beasts, as well as for all creatures whose habitat is marsh, swamp and river, mountain or plain. Besides all this, the earth bore freely all the aromatic substances it bears today, roots, herbs, bushes and gums exuded by flowers or fruit. There were cultivated crops, cereals which provide our staple diet, and pulse (to use its generic name) which we need in addition to feed us; there were the fruits of trees, hard to store but providing the drink and food and oil which give us pleasure and relaxation and which we serve after supper as a welcome refreshment to the weary when appetite is satisfied—all these were produced by that sacred island, then still beneath the sun, in wonderful quality and profusion.*

*This then was the island's natural endowment, and the inhabitants proceeded to build temples, palaces, harbours and docks, and to organize the country as a whole in the following manner.*

CRITIAS

The first settlement of the early Atlantans was on the Central Island, which they cleared and transformed into fertile arable and pasture land. The island was richly endowed with mineral resources, timber, game, and fruit, and irrigated by the warm and cold springs.

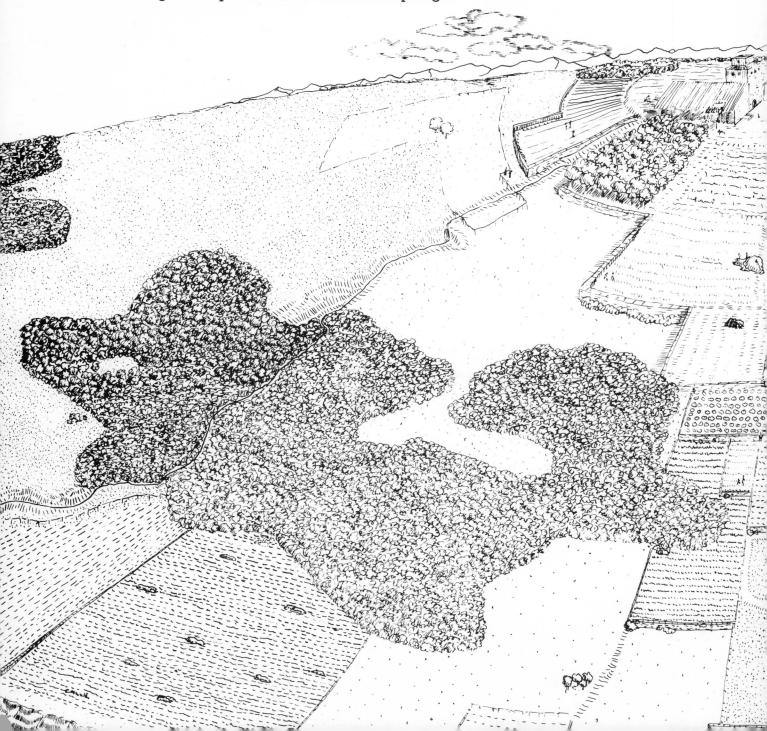

Orichalc is a mystery to us, as it was to Plato, who mentions it often. Even in his day it survived "only in name." The multipurpose "fruits of trees" could have been bananas or coconuts.

The luxuriant vegetation, the elephants, indicate the subtropical climate Atlantis enjoyed: the protected South Coast was warmed by the Gulf Stream.

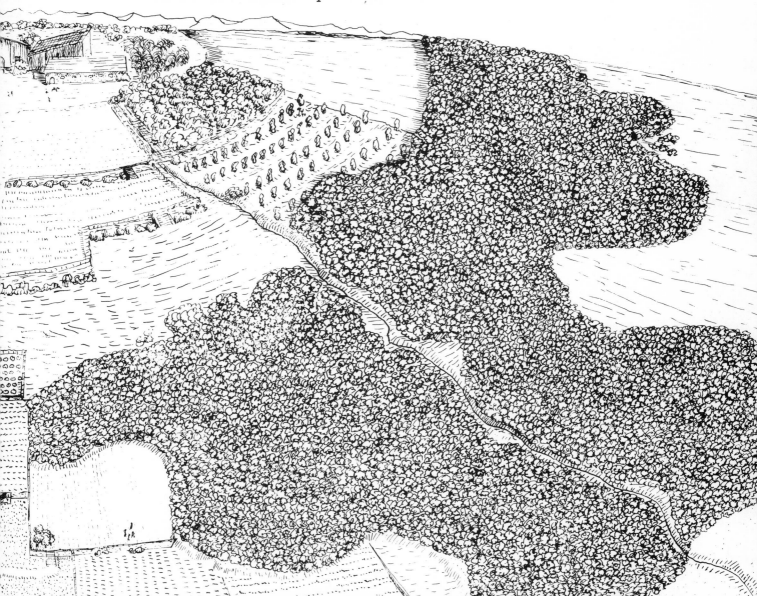

# THE CENTRAL ISLAND BEFORE THE CONSTRUCTION OF THE ACROPOLIS

# The Building of the Palace

*This palace they proceeded to build at once in the place where the god and their ancestors had lived, and each successive king added to its beauties, doing his best to surpass his predecessors, until they had made a residence whose size and beauty were astonishing to see. . . .*

*The construction of the palace within the acropolis was as follows. In the centre was a shrine sacred to Poseidon and Cleito, surrounded by a golden wall through which entry was forbidden, as it was the place where the family of the ten kings was conceived and begotten; and there year by year seasonal offerings were made from the ten provinces to each one of them.*

CRITIAS

The royal palace of Atlantis, built on the site of the house Poseidon and Cleito shared, was extended and improved by one ruler after another over a period of at least 2,500 years, and at its height must have been an incomparably magnificent sight, monumental and adorned with the wealth of a mighty empire. Its construction rivals—indeed, surpasses—the accomplishments of the pyramid builders. Like the Egyptians, the Atlantans undoubtedly used the expandable ramp for setting the huge stone blocks in position, but for the great columns this method would not suffice. Here perhaps their special abilities as hydraulic engineers were again put to use; these people well understood the power of water.

The system devised for the erection of the columns was simple but extremely clever. Each column, hewn in one piece out of rock, has a point of articulation and is rolled to its correct site on round poles (1), with the point of articulation placed directly above its bearing (2); ropes are attached near the top. The poles are burned and the column begins to tilt into position (3). A large container is affixed to the column and filled with water, and the weight thus created gradually pushes the column upward (4). Meanwhile, a scaffold is constructed for support (5). The column is slowly and carefully brought fully upright by adjusting the position and weight of the water container, and elephants pulling ropes assist by counterbalancing the column and keeping it from toppling forward (6).

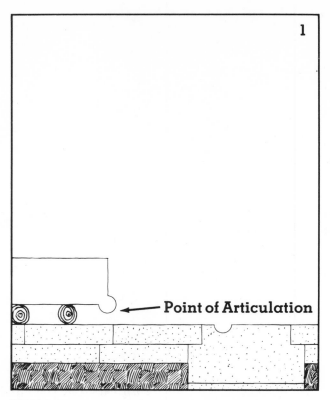

← **Point of Articulation**

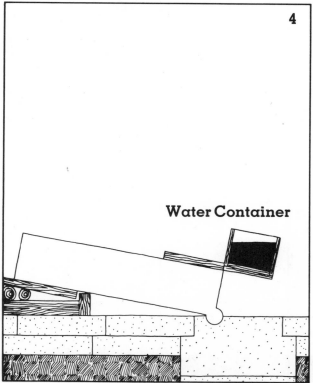

**Water Container**

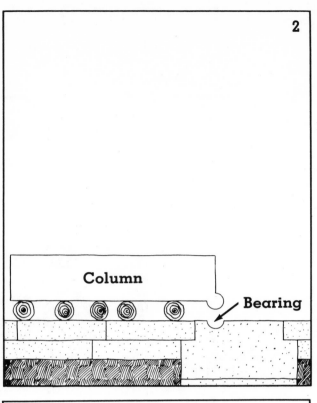

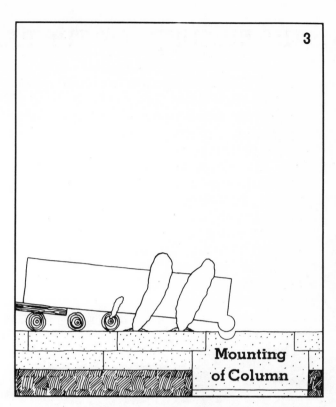

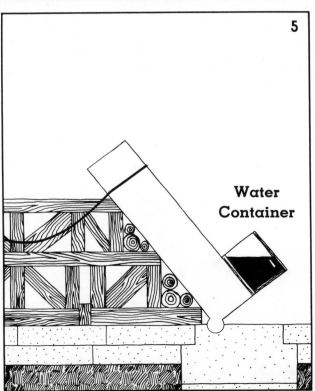

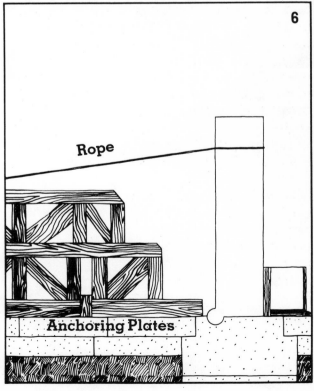

# THE BUILDING OF THE PALACE

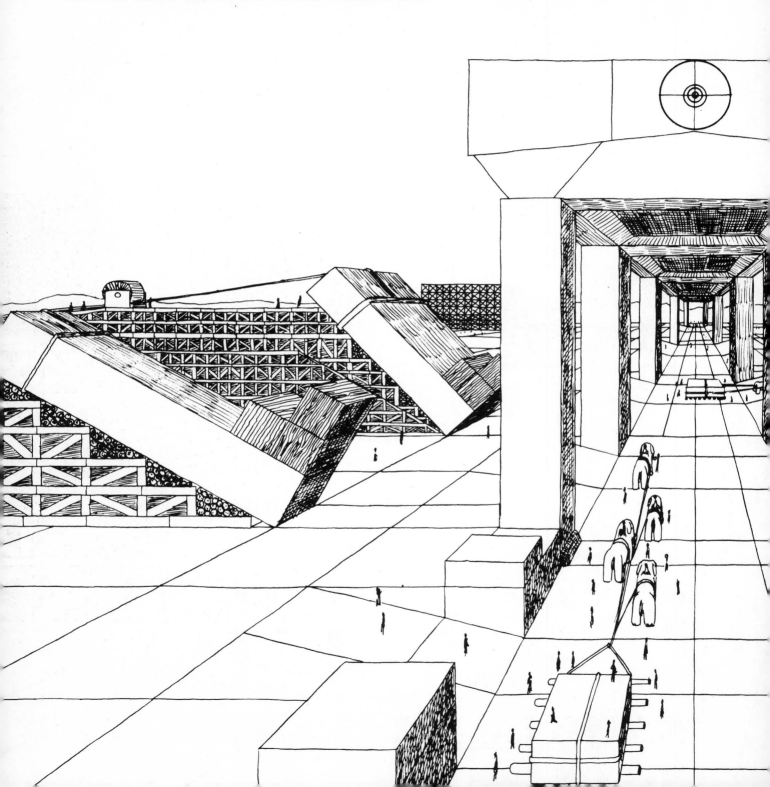

# The Construction of the Bridges

*Their first work was to bridge the rings of water round their mother's original home, so forming a road to and from their palace. . . . The largest of the rings, to which there was access from the sea, was three stades in breadth and the ring of land within it the same. Of the second pair the ring of water was two stades in breadth, and the ring of land again equal to it, while the ring of water running immediately round the central island was a stade across. The diameter of the island on which the palace was situated was five stades.*

CRITIAS

When the Atlantans finished building their palace, they began the task of bridging the three water belts. Plato gives their dimensions in stades, converted in the diagram below to yards:

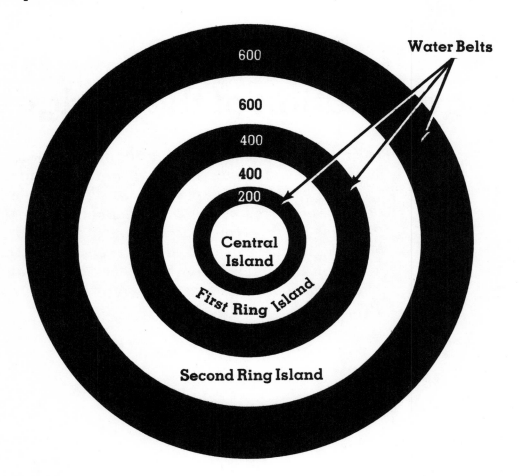

The diameter of the entire land and water belt system was a little over 3¼ miles.

The bridges were themselves a major achievement of Atlantan architecture. Thousands of workers were involved, and thousands more were building connecting roads and a water channel network for the warm and cold springs Poseidon had created on the Central Island.

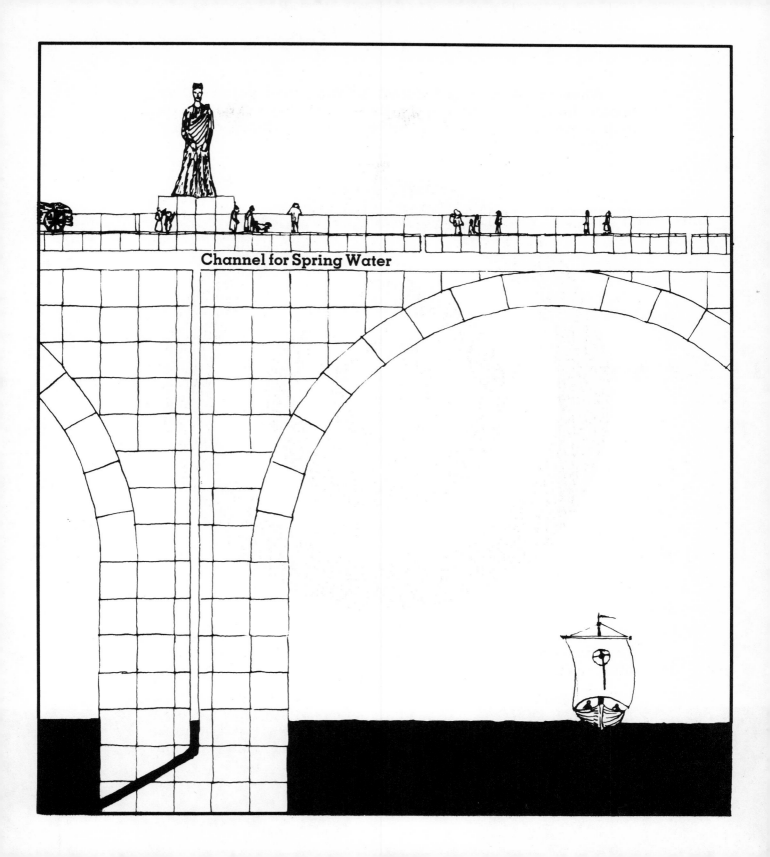

Channel for Spring Water

# BRIDGE AND TOWER

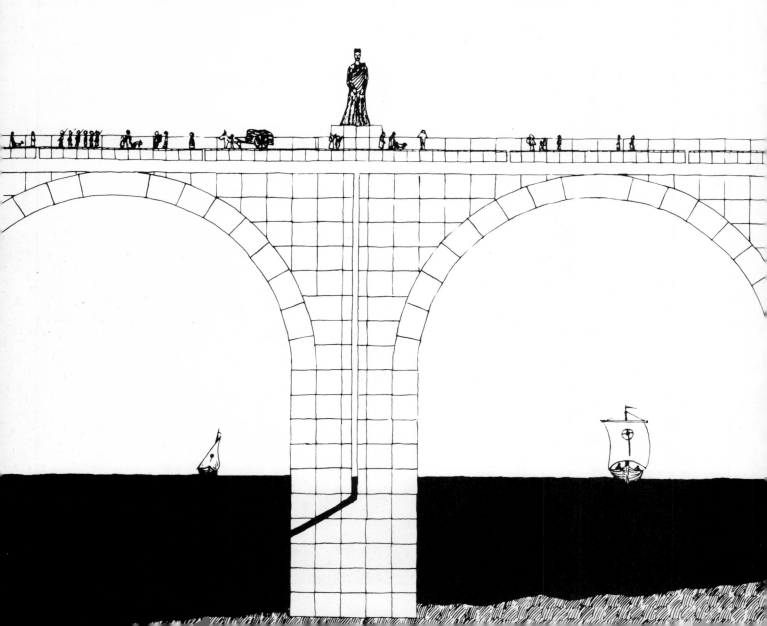

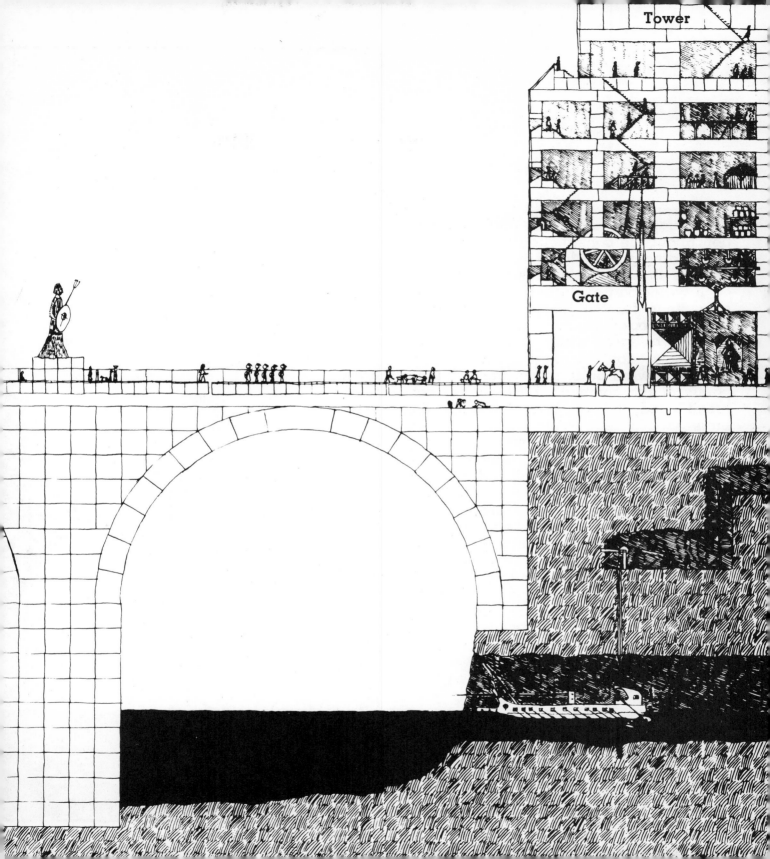

Tower

Gate

Although Plato gives no information about the construction method used in building the bridges, it seems fairly obvious that the Atlantans first drained each water belt and quarried the necessary stone for the bridges on the spot from the rocky ground.

The bridges, which also served as aqueducts for drinking water and drainage, were built at the four cardinal points of the compass. Each is 100 feet broad, and the distance between the piers is 138 feet; each bridgehead is crowned by a mighty tower. Subterranean channels through which ships could move from one ring of water to another begin beneath the last pair of girders. The bridges were embellished with large statues of gods and kings.

About 100,000 workers were involved in this project—surveyors, engineers, geometricians, architects, foremen, toolmasters, laborers—and hundreds of elephants. Perfect organization was required to coordinate and sustain such a vast undertaking.

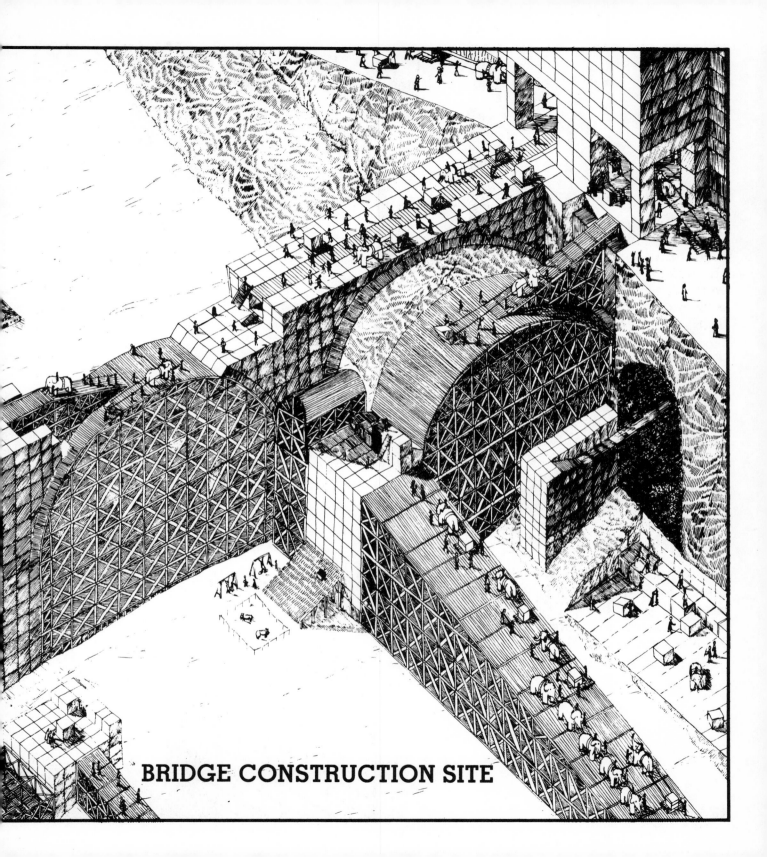

BRIDGE CONSTRUCTION SITE

# The Subterranean Channels and Docks

At the bridges they made channels through the rings of land which separated those of water, large enough to admit the passage of a single trireme, and roofed over to make an underground tunnel; for the rims of the rings were of some height above sea-level.

CRITIAS

The Atlantans not only built bridges to connect the plain, the Ring Islands, and the Central Island, they also connected the water belts with one another by means of subterranean channels. The longer of these was 600 yards (the width of the larger Ring Island), the shorter 400 yards. Both ran in line with the bridges on the north-south axis. On the channel under the larger Ring Island there were various underground stations for loading and unloading both passengers and goods of all kinds.

The construction method the Atlantans used for the channels was surely the same as that employed by the Romans. First the channel was measured and laid out on land. Then shafts were dug at regular intervals down to the level of the channel. These shafts had three purposes: they served as points of orientation for the surveyors, they were used for transport of workers and material, and they provided ventilation. The rock removed from the shafts and the channel bed was carefully hewn and transported via ramps and the drained water belts to other construction sites.

The channel through the small Ring Island could be mined and thus built underground. However, the larger land belt was for the most part not high enough above the water line for tunneling and underground construction. So, that channel had to be built in the open, filled with water, and then covered—and covered securely, since above it would be laid out the race course!

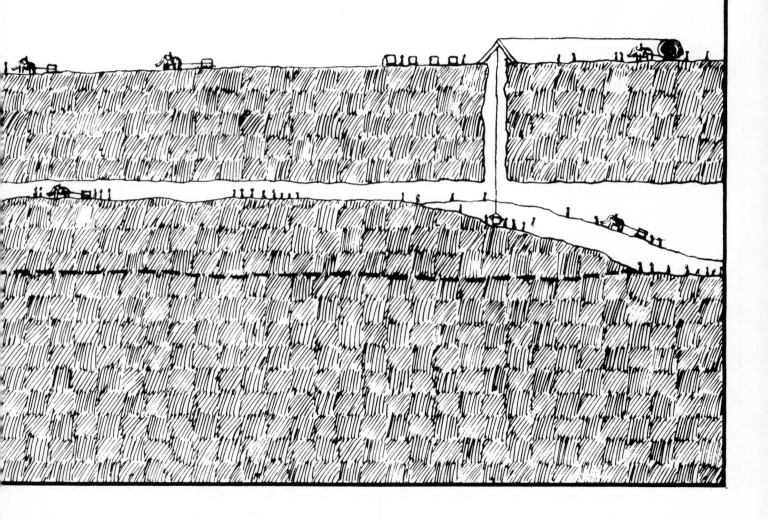

# CONSTRUCTION OF CHANNEL UNDER LARGER RING ISLAND

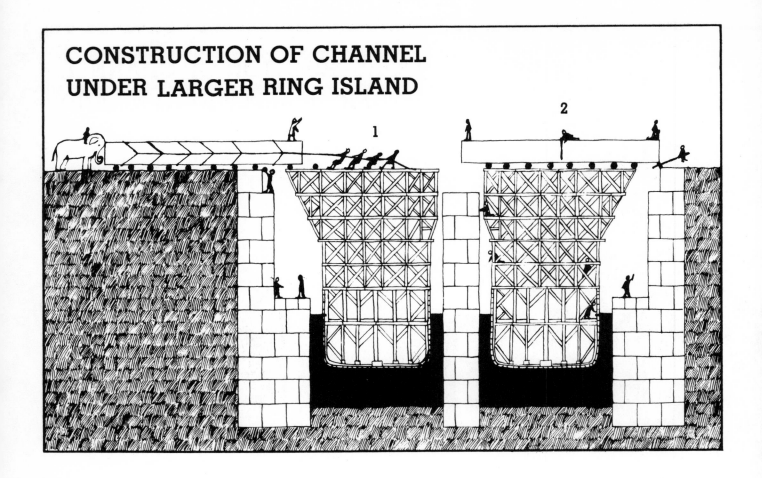

Plato reported that the channels were wide enough for a trireme, a Greek warship about 20 feet wide. To allow sufficient clearance for the oars on both sides, the channels were at least 50 feet across. Horses and elephants probably pulled the ships through the channels, so there must have been towpaths alongside. Wood of course would not be strong enough to roof over the channels and paths, so the Atlantans used stone slabs.

Even if each of these slabs was only 3 feet square in cross section, because of the immense span it would have weighed about 60 tons. I asked myself how these could have been put in place. We know how the Egyptions and Romans transported stone slabs of similar dimensions on land. Again, I believe the particular talents of the Atlantans as hydraulic engineers and as shipbuilders came into play. In the following illustrations I show a simple and practicable method that I think would have appealed to them.

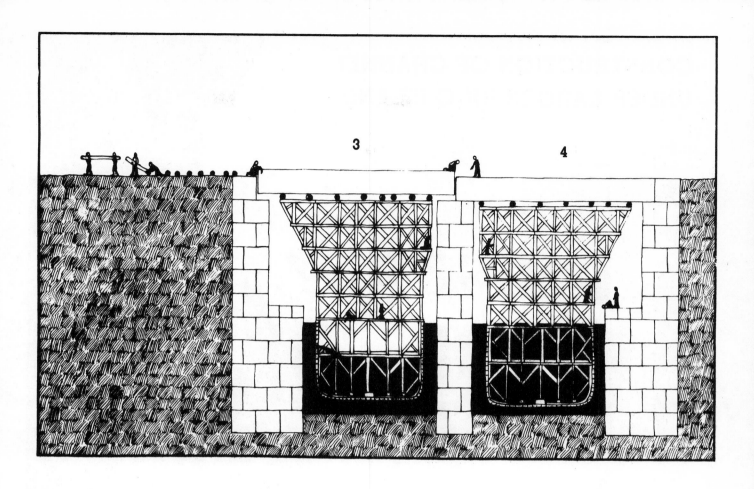

First, the slabs are rolled on round timbers to the open channel and rolled onto a scaffold carried by a ship standing in the channel (1). When the slab is in position on the scaffold, a diver opens a valve below the water line and compartments of the ship bearing the scaffold slowly fill with water (2). As the ship continues to fill, it rides lower in the water and the slab is lowered into place; the ship is then lowered slightly further to allow clearance (3). With the slab in position and the ship clear, a diver closes the valve (4). Then the boat is towed away, pumped out, and brought round to be ready to receive the next slab.

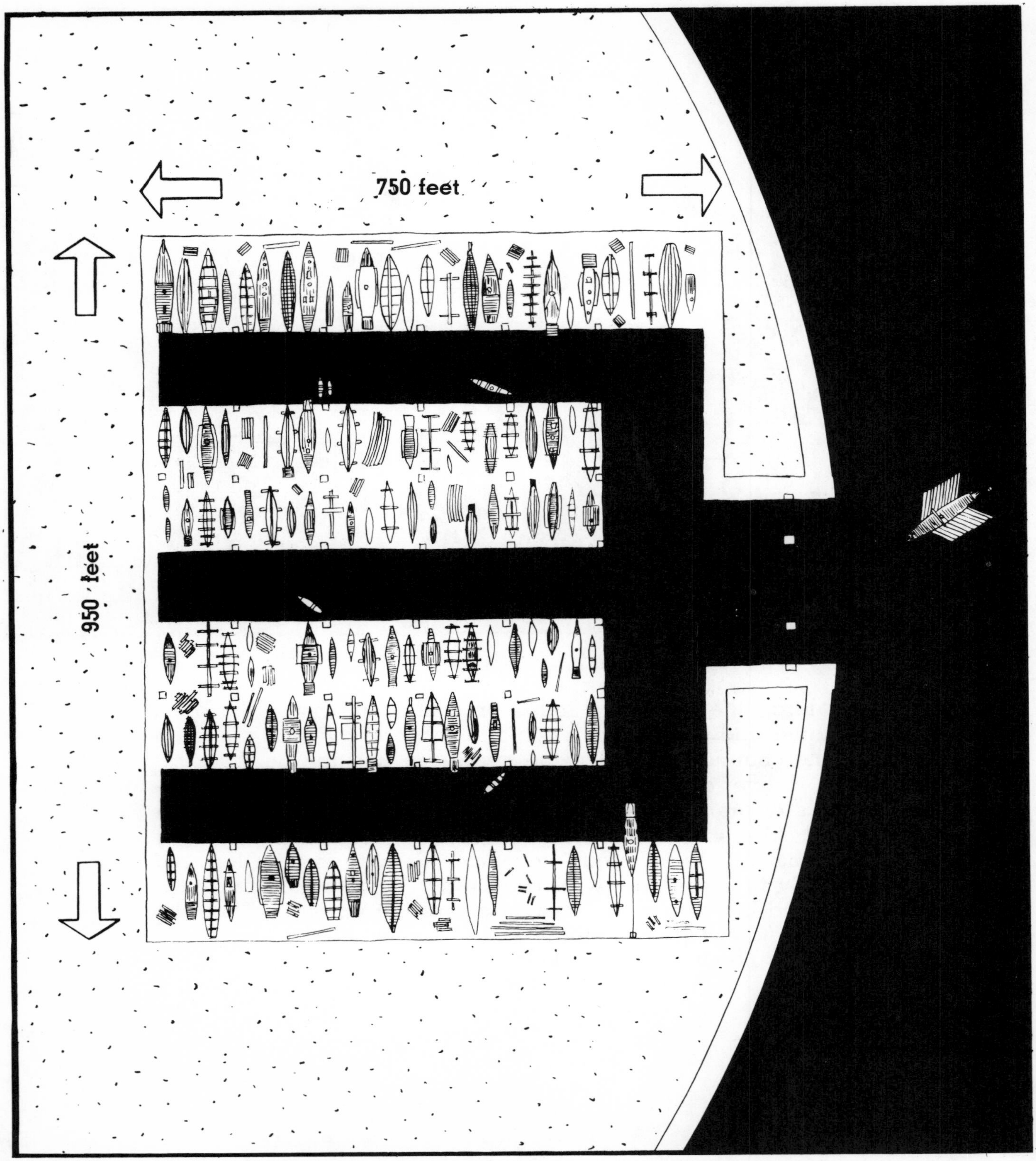
750 feet
950 feet

The subterranean channels led to underground docks built in a rock cave beneath the Central Island. The empire of Atlantis was a sea empire, with a navy of 1,200 ships. Both for defense and trade, control of the sea was paramount.

The docks had berths for 130 ships arranged as shown, in an overall area of more than 16 acres.

Six 650-foot wharves accommodated the construction of warships and merchant vessels as well as repair work of all kinds. When the vast underground marina was built the stone was carefully excavated and subsequently used in the construction of walls and towers on the surface.

THE UNDERGROUND DOCKS

# The Temple of Poseidon

*There was a temple of Poseidon himself, a stade in length, three hundred feet wide and proportionate in height, though somewhat outlandish in appearance. The outside of it was covered all over with silver, except for the figures on the pediment which were covered with gold. Inside, the roof was ivory picked out with gold, silver and orichalc, and all the walls, pillars and floor were covered with orichalc. It contained gold statues of the god standing in a chariot drawn by six winged horses, so tall that his head touched the roof, and round him, riding on dolphins, a hundred Nereids (that being the accepted number of them at the time), as well as many other statues dedicated by private persons. Round the temple were statues of the original ten kings and their wives, and many others dedicated by kings and private persons belonging to the city and its dominions. There was an altar of a size and workmanship to match that of the building and a palace equally worthy of the greatness of the empire and the magnificence of its temples.*

CRITIAS

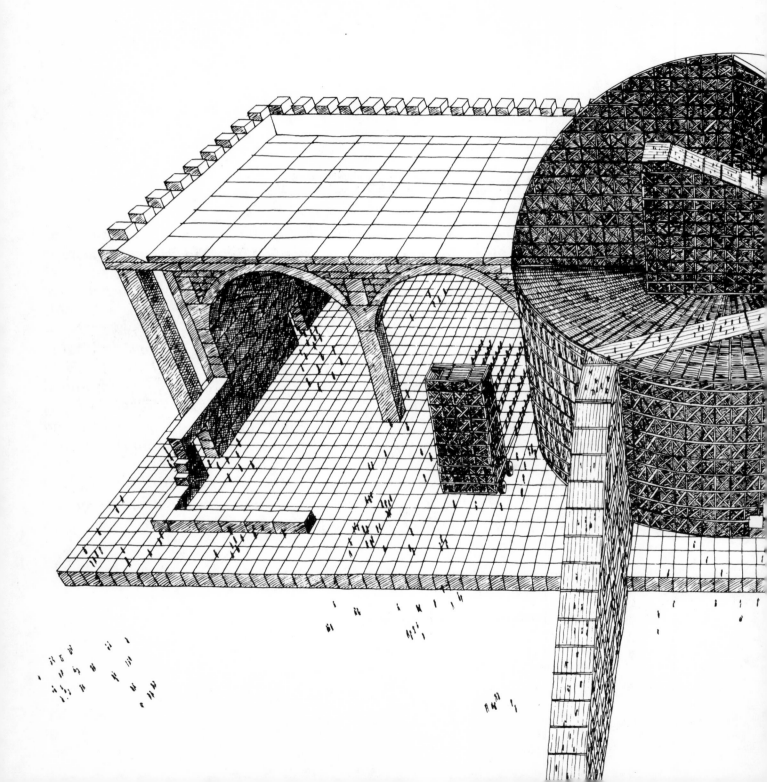

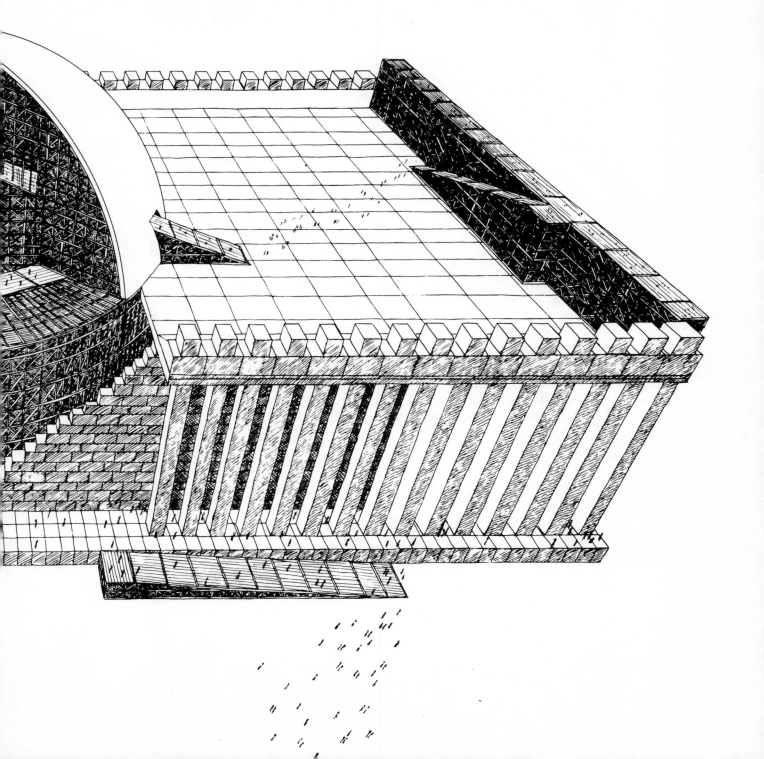

The Temple of Poseidon was the largest, most beautiful, and the most costly building in the Atlantan Empire. Though its proportions were balanced, they were so colossal—and its ornamentation so opulent—the Greek Plato was driven to call it *barbarikon*, "outlandish." It stood exactly in the center of the Acropolis on the Central Island and thus also in the center of the city of Atlantis. Its dimensions were gigantic: its floor area was about a third that of the Cheops Pyramid, the top of its cupola rose half as high as the Empire State Building. The statue of the god was of similar huge proportions. Standing on the highest point of the city, covered with gold, the cupola must have radiated an extraordinary light—what a beacon to the ships arriving from morning till night!

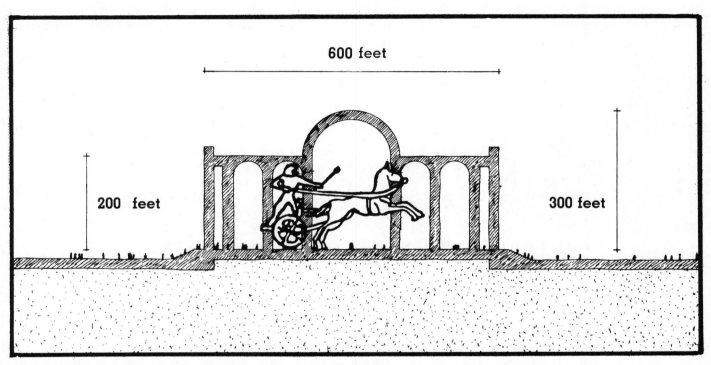

600 feet

200 feet

300 feet

# CROSS SECTION OF THE TEMPLE OF POSEIDON

# The Completed Acropolis

*The two springs, cold and hot, provided an unlimited supply of water for appropriate purposes, remarkable for its agreeable quality and excellence; and this they made available by surrounding it with suitable buildings and plantations, leading some of it into basins in the open air and some of it into covered hot baths for winter use. Here separate accommodation was provided for royalty and for commoners, and, again, for women, for horses and for other beasts of burden, appropriately equipped in each case.*
CRITIAS

The springs, housed in their own water temples, flowed on either side of the Temple of Poseidon, the cold water spring on the east and the warm on the west. These two side temples thus extended the façade of Poseidon's sanctuary, already as we know most impressive. The façades of the two water temples were reflected in pools that surrounded them and lent variation to the temple plaza. This huge square, a quarter of a mile on a side, was ornamented with scores of colossal statues carved of marble.

Immediately south of the Temple of Poseidon stood the palace, in a setting of luxuriant parks and gardens. Clad in the finest and most colorful varieties of marble, the palace was built on both sides of the main road leading from the first water belt to the temple plaza, the two wings connecting at the level of the second floor; thus a kind of arcade was formed. As well as housing the royal family (the royal apartments were on the upper floors), the palace complex provided accommodation and offices for staff, administrators, and other officials; guardroom and stables were in the basement.

This Acropolis, perhaps the richest the world has known, must have given Atlantan and visitor alike an almost palpable sense of the glory and might of Atlantis.

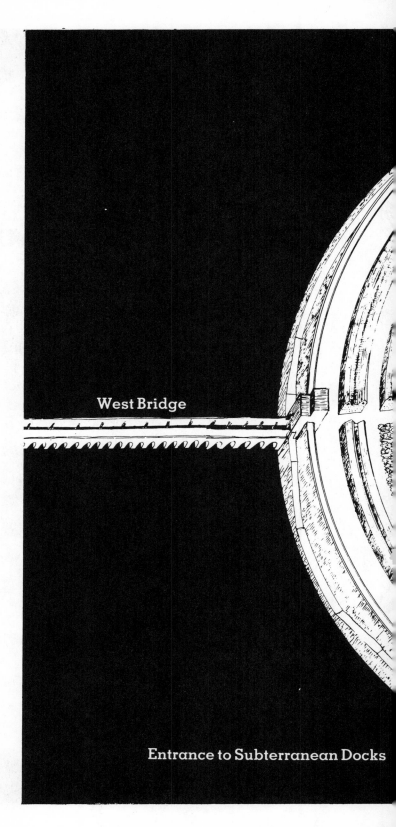

West Bridge

Entrance to Subterranean Docks

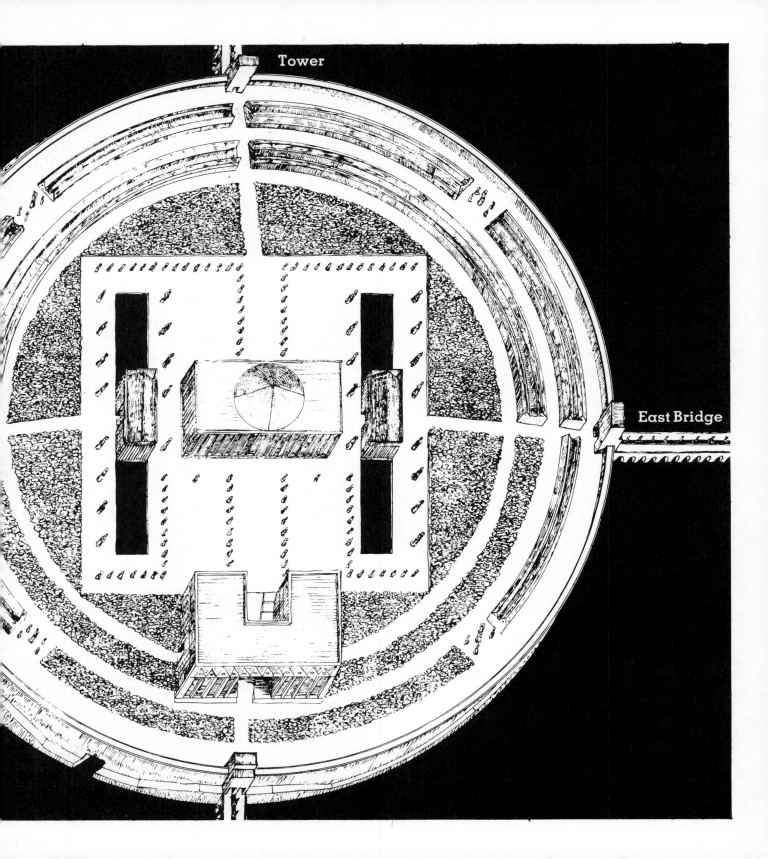

Tower

East Bridge

# The Completed Ring Islands

*The outflow they led into the grove of Poseidon, which (because of the goodness of the soil) was full of trees of marvellous beauty and height, and also channelled it to the outer ring-islands by aqueducts at the bridges. On each of these ring-islands they had built many temples for different gods, and many gardens and areas for exercise, some for men and some for horses. On the middle of the larger island in particular there was a special course for horse-racing; its width was a stade and its length that of a complete circuit of the island, which was reserved for it. Round it on both sides were barracks for the main body of the king's body-guard. A more select body of the more trustworthy were stationed on the smaller island ring nearer the citadel, and the most trustworthy of all had quarters assigned to them in the citadel and were attached to the king's person.*

*Finally, there were dockyards full of triremes and their equipment, all in good shape.*

*So much then for the arrangement of the royal residence and its environs.*

CRITIAS

While the water belts were drained to facilitate construction of the bridges, work was being done on the Ring Islands and the city of Atlantis began to take shape. On the small land belt, the first Ring Island, the splendid three-level Grove of Poseidon emerged, landscaped into a magnificent park. The larger land belt was the site of the race course; thickly forested, it was cleared by felling or burning the trees. So that races could take place without interruption, four bridges spanned the track, in line with the bridges over the water belts.

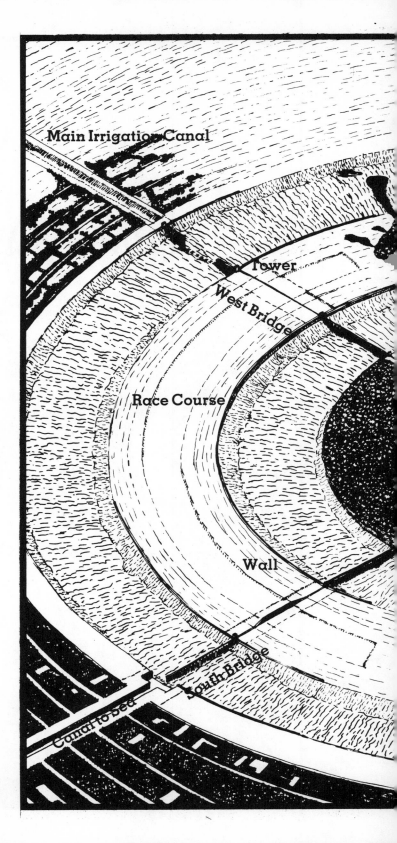

Main Irrigation Canal

Tower

West Bridge

Race Course

Wall

South Bridge

Canal to Sea

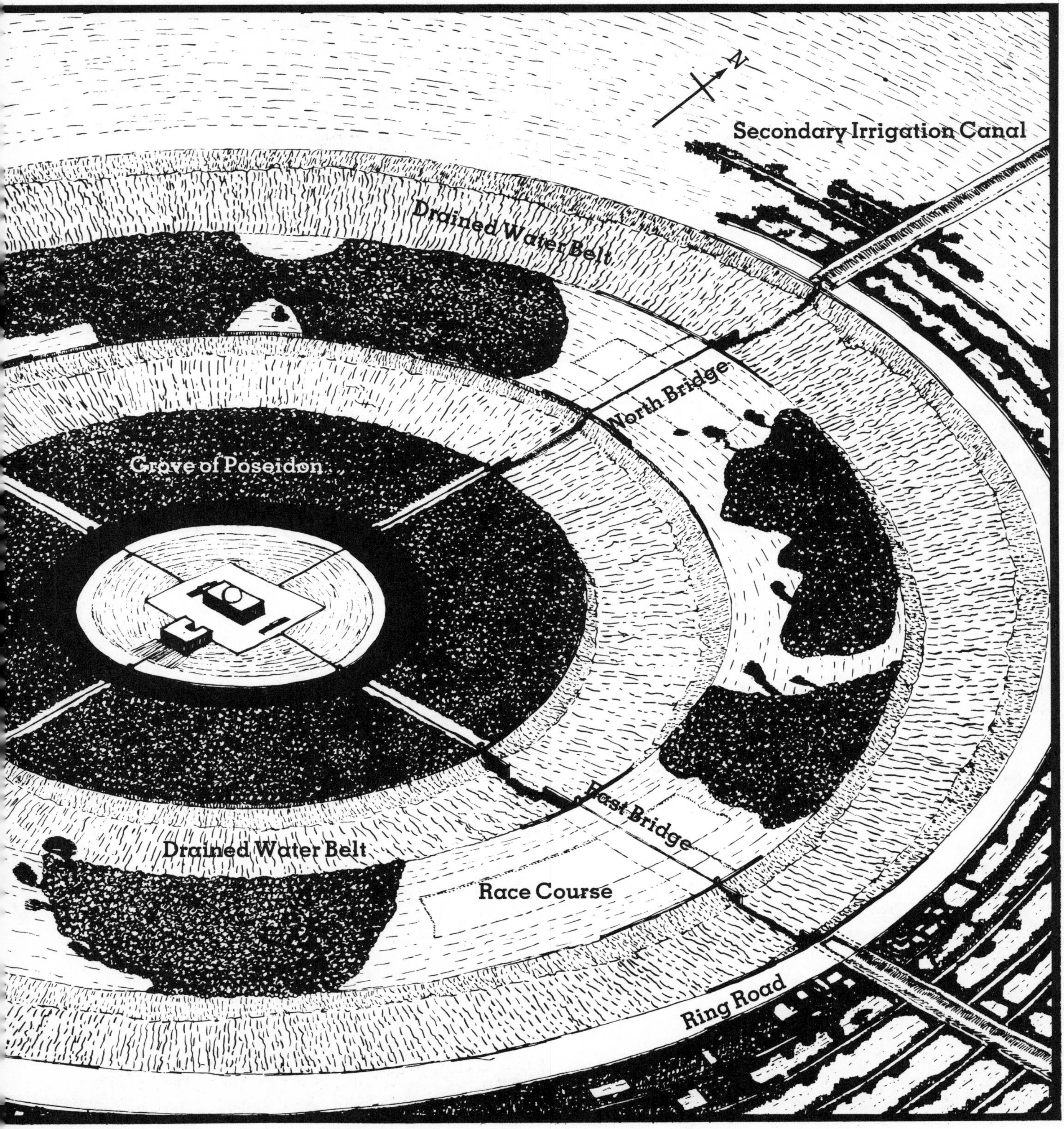

Secondary Irrigation Canal

Drained Water Belt

North Bridge

Grove of Poseidon

East Bridge

Drained Water Belt

Race Course

Ring Road

The races started and finished in front of the royal grandstand, from which projected the winner's rostrum. Ramps permitted riders and charioteers to appear on the rostrum without dismounting. The start-finish building was in the middle of the track, in front of the royal grandstand. Beyond it stood the victors' temple.

Just east of the royal grandstand the track was spanned by the North Bridge (under construction in the drawing). Under the approaches to the North Bridge on both sides of the track were stations of the subterranean channel.

Six hundred feet wide—equivalent to a thirty-lane highway—and about 8½ miles long, the race course was used not only for chariot, horse, and elephant races, but also as a parade ground and exercise area for the army, which was quartered in barracks concentric with the race track and on both sides of it.

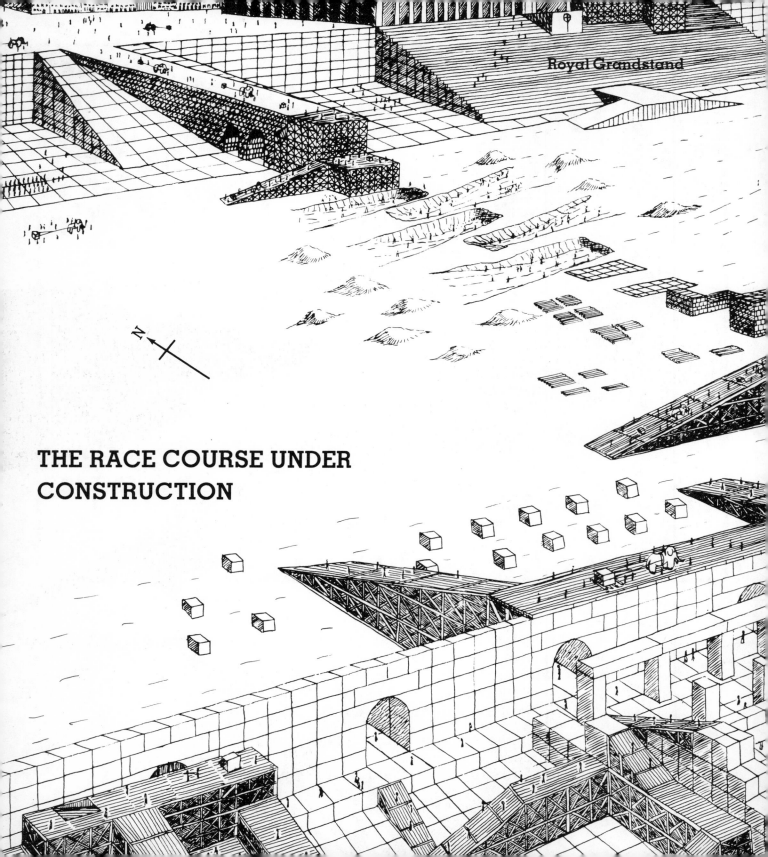

Royal Grandstand

N

THE RACE COURSE UNDER
CONSTRUCTION

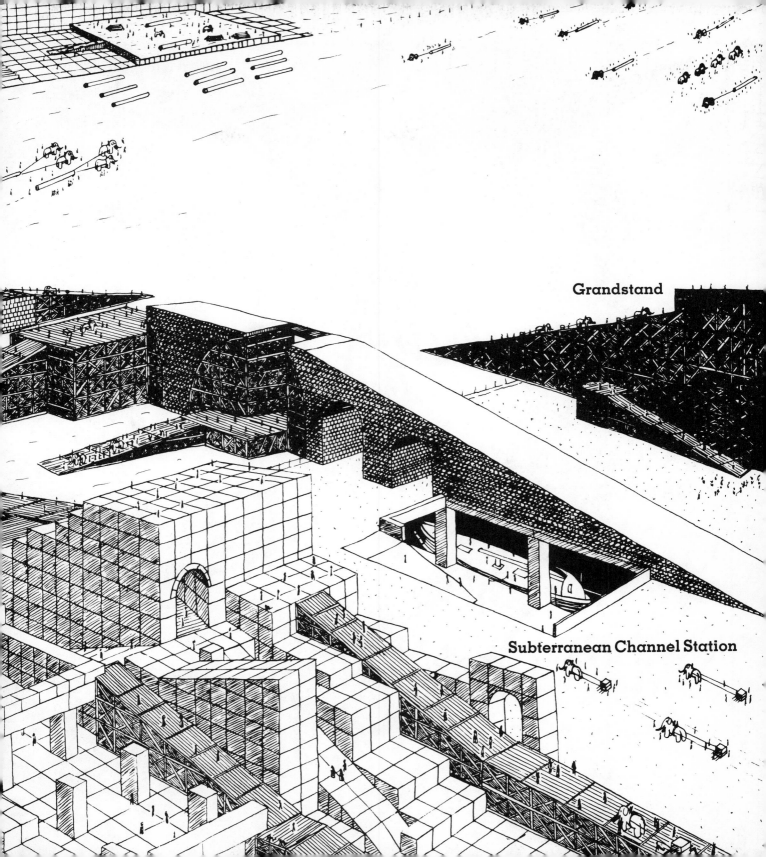

Grandstand

Subterranean Channel Station

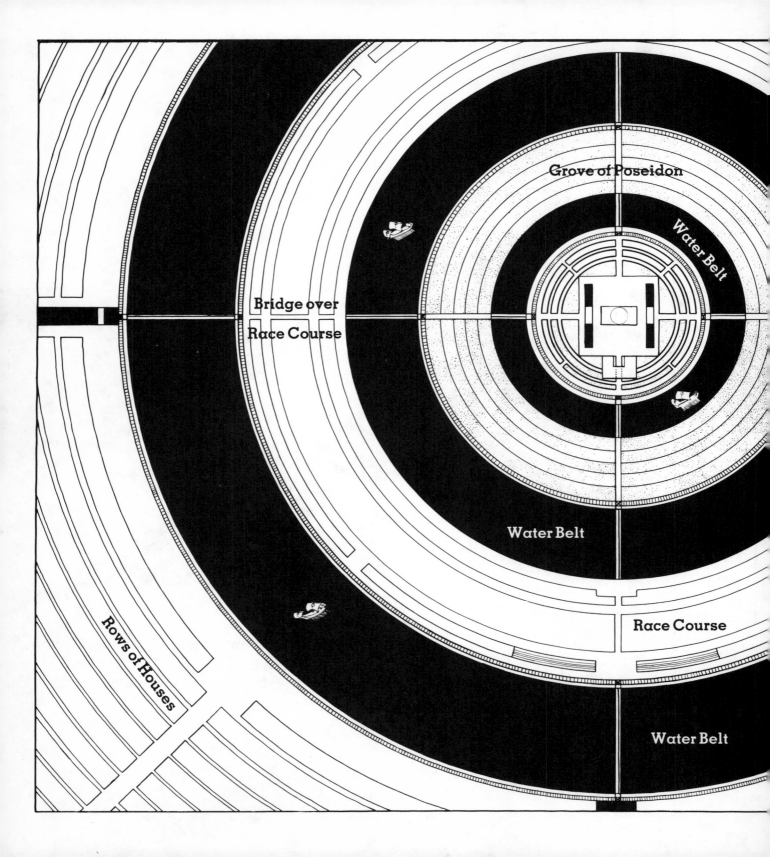

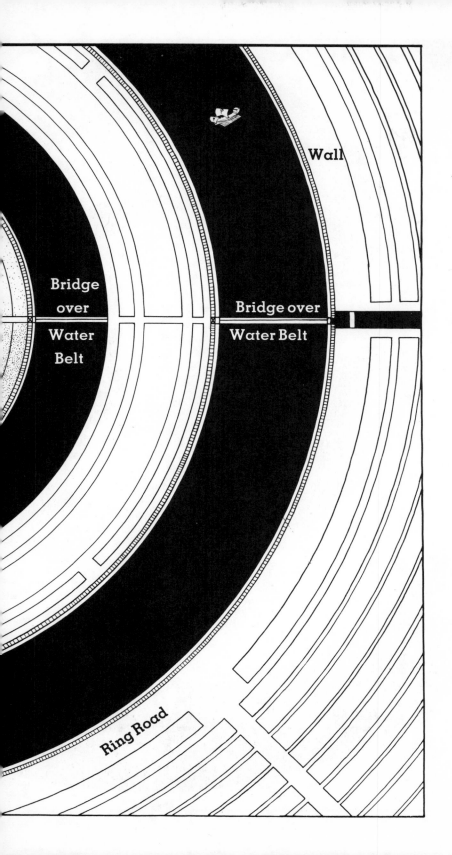

Bridge
over
Water
Belt

Bridge over
Water Belt

Wall

Ring Road

# The Canal to the Sea

*They began by digging a canal three hundred feet wide, a hundred feet deep and fifty stades long from the sea to the outermost ring, thus making it accessible from the sea like a harbour; and they made the entrance to it large enough to admit the largest ships.*

CRITIAS

With the Acropolis finished and the bridges in place, the Atlantans were ready to begin work on the canal from the sea to the outermost water belt. Again Plato gives us dimensions: the canal was 300 feet wide, 100 feet deep and a little more than 5½ miles long.

At the sea end of the canal the Atlantans built a system of double sluices with an overflow to regulate the water level. About 1¼ miles farther inland, there was a small port in a basin of about 650 feet by 1,300 feet. The larger harbor, some five-eighths of a mile nearer the city, is about twice that size, or a quarter of a mile square.

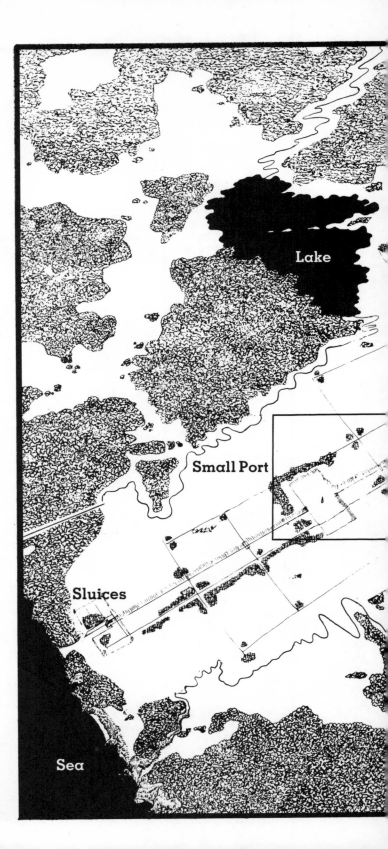

Lake

Small Port

Sluices

Sea

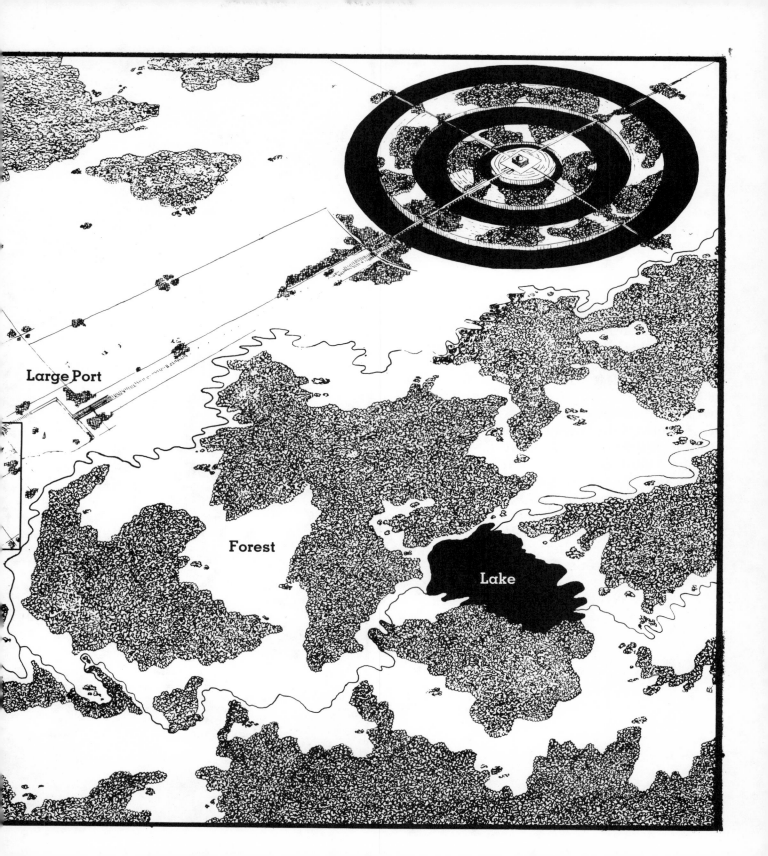

Large Port

Forest

Lake

The outlined area on the previous drawing is now enlarged to show in greater detail the construction site for the small harbor. Along the Ring Road, in the upper left, are seen foundations for houses; the surveyor's pickets in the lower right align other Ring Roads to be built. Just above these are the construction headquarters, and when the canal is complete and operational this building will house the port administration. At the four corners of the harbor itself seafarers' temples are built. When the harbor is finished and filled with water, the surveyor's obelisk will serve as marker and ornament.

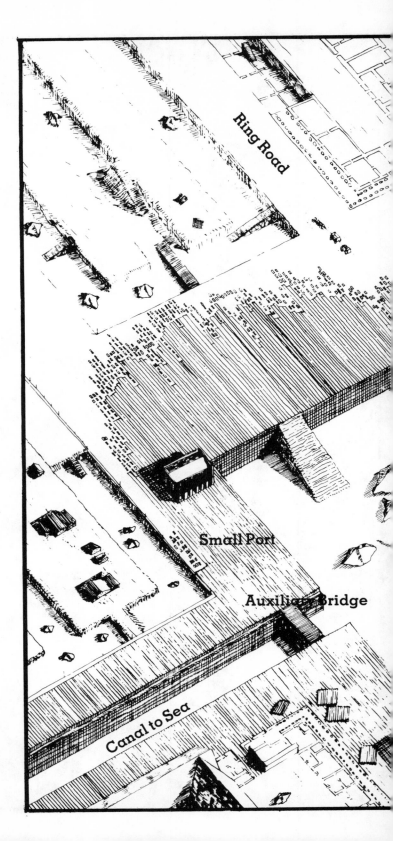

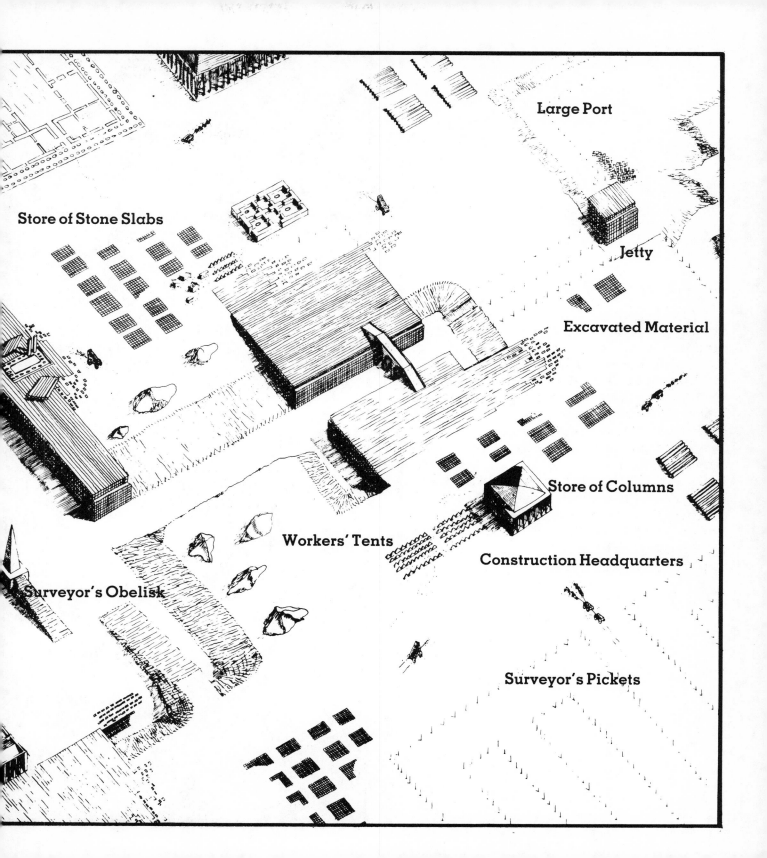

Large Port

Store of Stone Slabs

Jetty

Excavated Material

Store of Columns

Workers' Tents

Construction Headquarters

Surveyor's Obelisk

Surveyor's Pickets

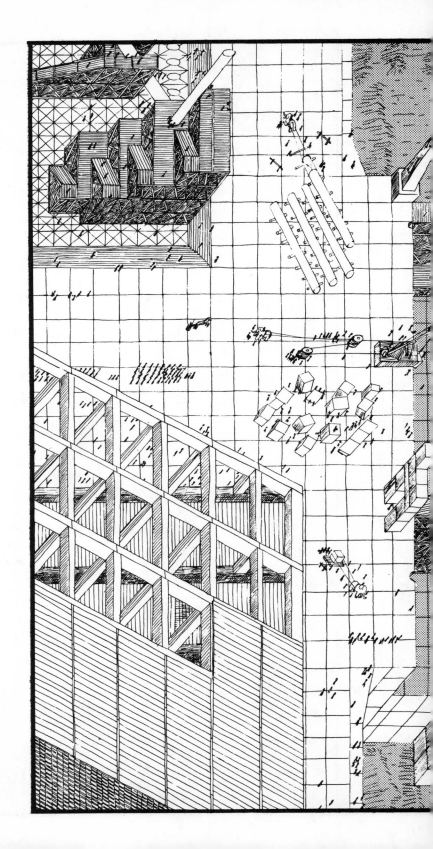

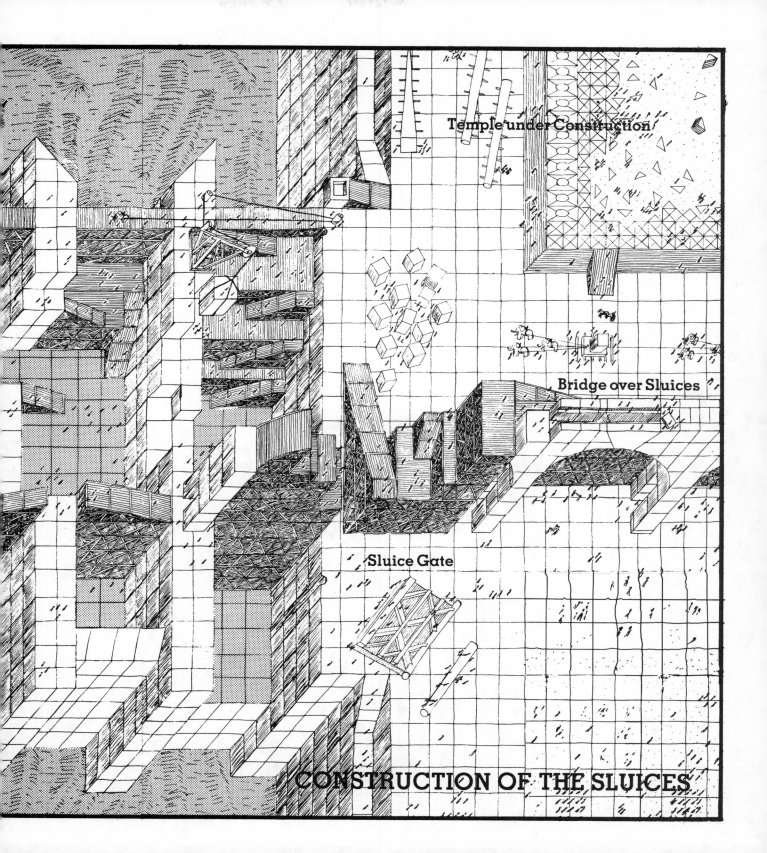

Temple under Construction

Bridge over Sluices

Sluice Gate

CONSTRUCTION OF THE SLUICES

300 feet

While the canal was under construction, the Ring Road system was built to complete the transportation network. Sixty-six Ring Roads, four of them major thoroughfares, circle the city, crossed by eight roads radiating out like spokes of a wheel from the outermost water belt, and another eight from the second major Ring Road to the city wall.

**RING ROAD SYSTEM**

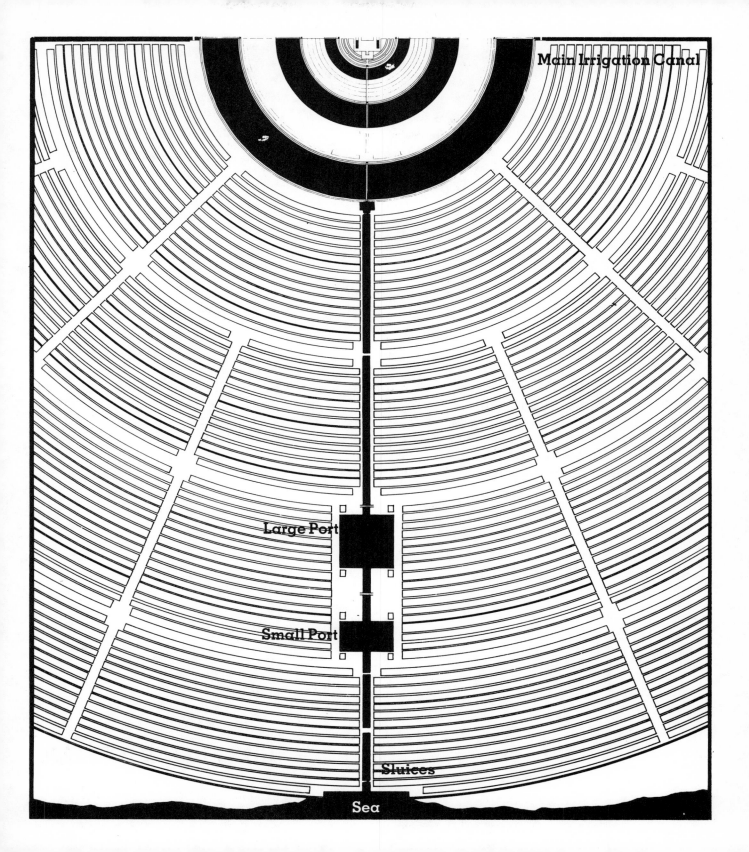

# The Walls and the Towers

*It [the Central Island] and the rings and the bridges (which were a hundred feet broad) were enclosed by a stone wall all round, with towers and gates guarding the bridges on either side where they crossed the water. The stone for them, which was white, black and yellow, they cut out of the central island and the outer and inner rings of land, and in the process excavated pairs of hollow docks with roofs of rock. Some of their buildings were of a single colour, in others they mixed different coloured stone to divert the eye and afford them appropriate pleasure. And they covered the whole circuit of the outermost wall with a veneer of bronze, they fused tin over the inner wall and orichalc gleaming like fire over the wall of the acropolis itself. . . .*

*Beyond the three outer harbours there was a wall, beginning at the sea and running right round in a circle, at a uniform distance of fifty stades from the largest ring and harbour and returning on itself at the mouth of the canal to the sea. This wall was densely built up all round with houses and the canal and large harbour were crowded with vast numbers of merchant ships from all quarters, from which rose a constant din of shouting and noise day and night.*

CRITIAS

93

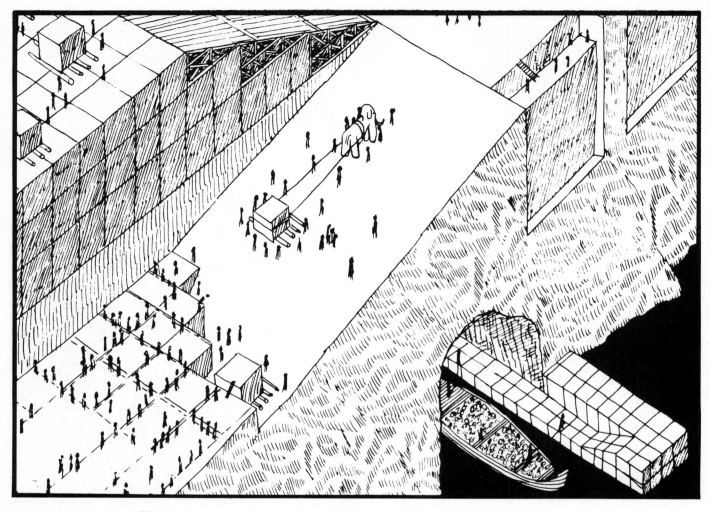

Thus four great walls enclosed the city of Atlantis in concentric circles. The Acropolis was walled, as were the two Ring Islands, and the whole city was protected by the outermost wall, whose radius was the distance from the Acropolis to the sea.

The aggregate length of the walls was almost 50 miles; they were 50 feet broad, and twice as high. To build them, and their gates and towers, was a feat as impressive as the construction of the canals.

The quantity of stone required was roughly 27 times that used in an Egyptian pyramid. So the engineers and construction supervisors were especially mindful of the question of materials and transport: the shorter the distance between the quarry and the building site, the faster construction work could proceed.

For the walls, towers, and gates around the Central Island and the Ring Islands, the Atlantans hewed building stone from the rocky coasts. Natural ramps were created by hewing the blocks at an angle. In this way the Atlantans achieved speed and the opportunity to trim and shape their coastline.

In the far right of the following drawing, stone blocks are being quarried from the coastline. The blocks were probably broken off by means of wooden wedges inserted in cracks and then wetted until they swelled. In the center, the large white surface is the foundation slab for a gate tower. Below it the anchorage for the connection of the bridge girders has already been built, and near it a subterranean channel. At top left, the road is under construction; on either side of it run the channels for the cold and warm water springs, and drainage channels.

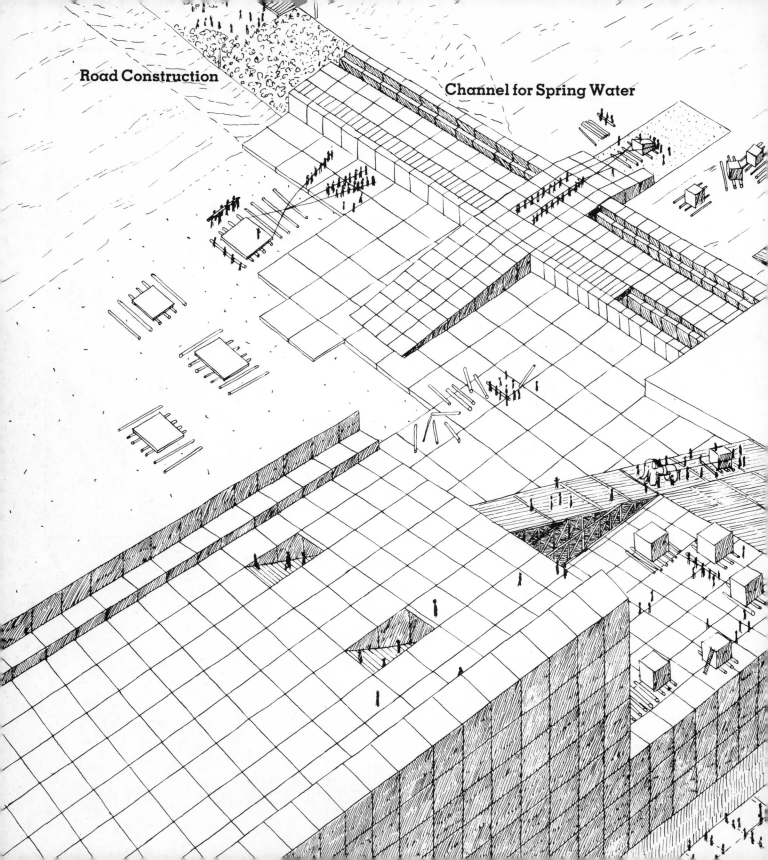

Road Construction

Channel for Spring Water

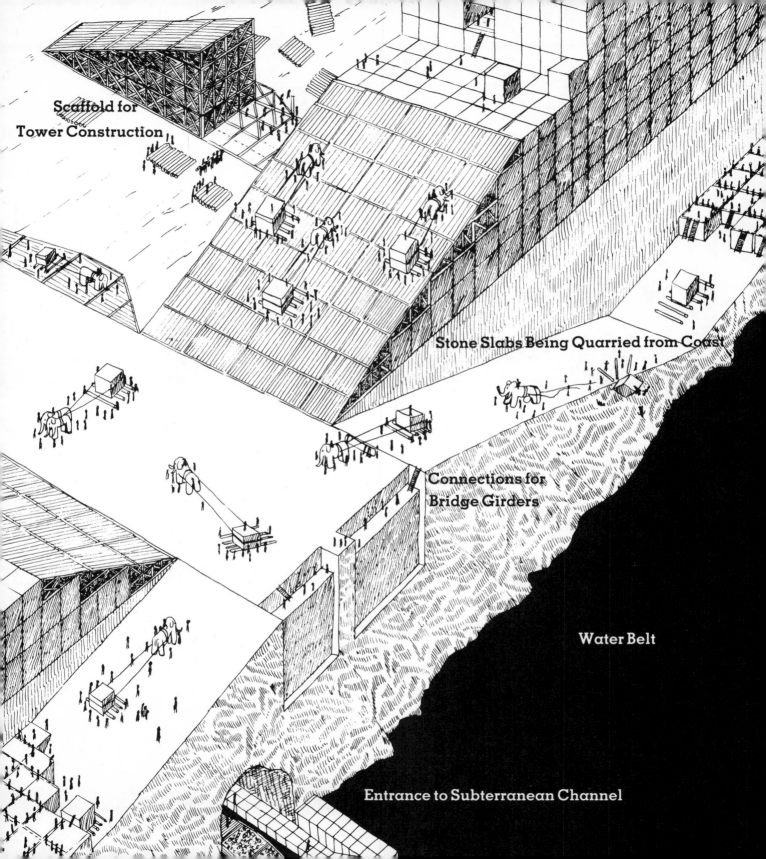

Scaffold for
Tower Construction

Stone Slabs Being Quarried from Coast

Connections for
Bridge Girders

Water Belt

Entrance to Subterranean Channel

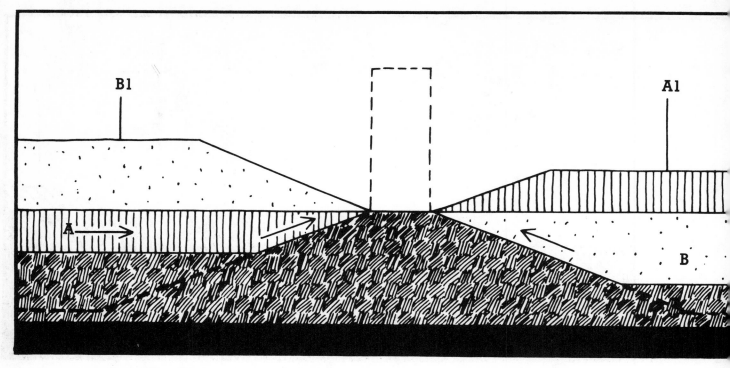

The hewn stone slabs (A) were transported by elephants via ramps to the building site (A1). Sections B and C were similarly constructed.

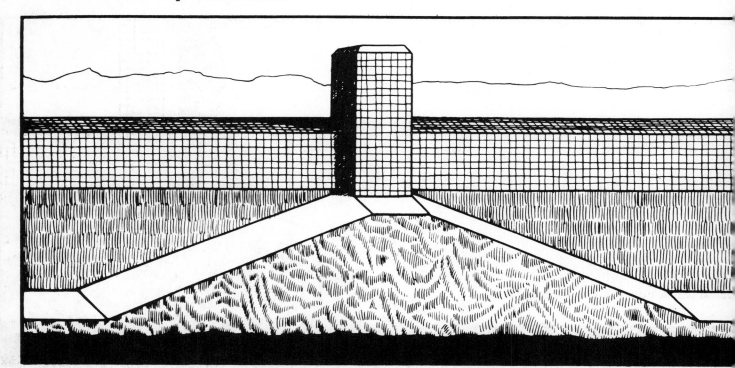

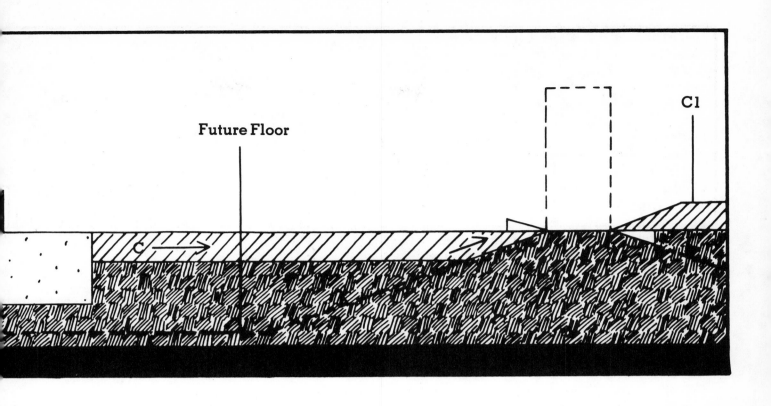

Future Floor

C1

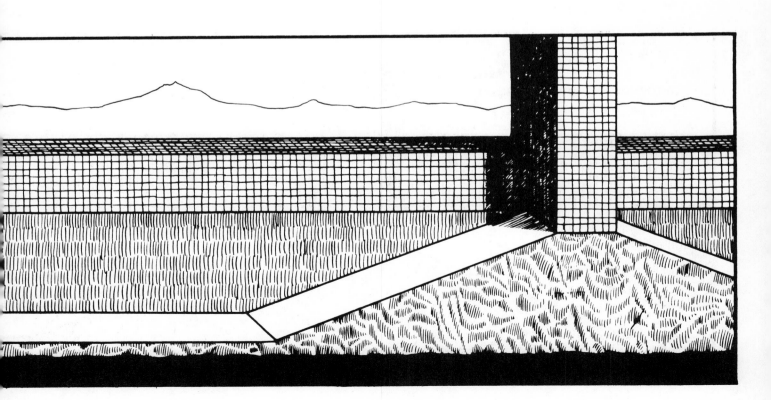

The walls were beautiful as well as imposing. The stone was not dull gray, but brilliant whites, blacks, yellows. The innermost wall, that surrounding the Acropolis, was clad with the mystery metal, orichalc—whatever it was, it "gleamed like fire." The wall surrounding the Grove of Poseidon on the first Ring Island was embellished with tin, and bronze covered the wall around the larger Ring Island, on which the race course was situated. The longest wall of all, the one enclosing the entire city, was a continuous mosaic built of different colored stones.

The metal coverings for the three inner walls were applied to the stones before construction. The rough-hewn blocks (square for the main body of the wall, triangular for the beveled edges), were first rolled to a central foundry. There the blocks were cut to exact shape and embedded in sand which was dug out around them to form molds. Molten metal—orichalc, tin, or bronze—was poured into the sand mold around the stone. When the metal coat had hardened on the stone, the stone was dug out and transported to the building site. When the wall was standing the outer, metal-clad surfaces were polished so that the different metals appeared in their full majesty, sparkling in the sunlight.

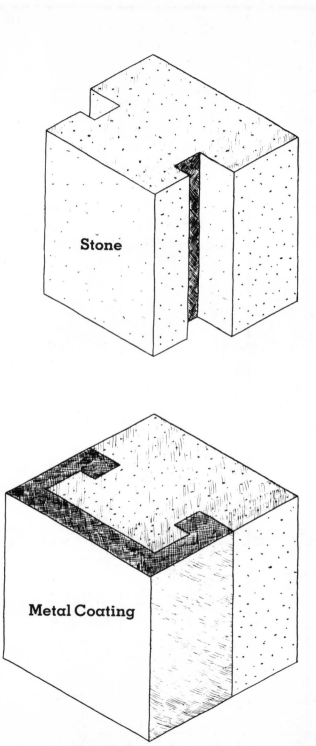

Stone

Metal Coating

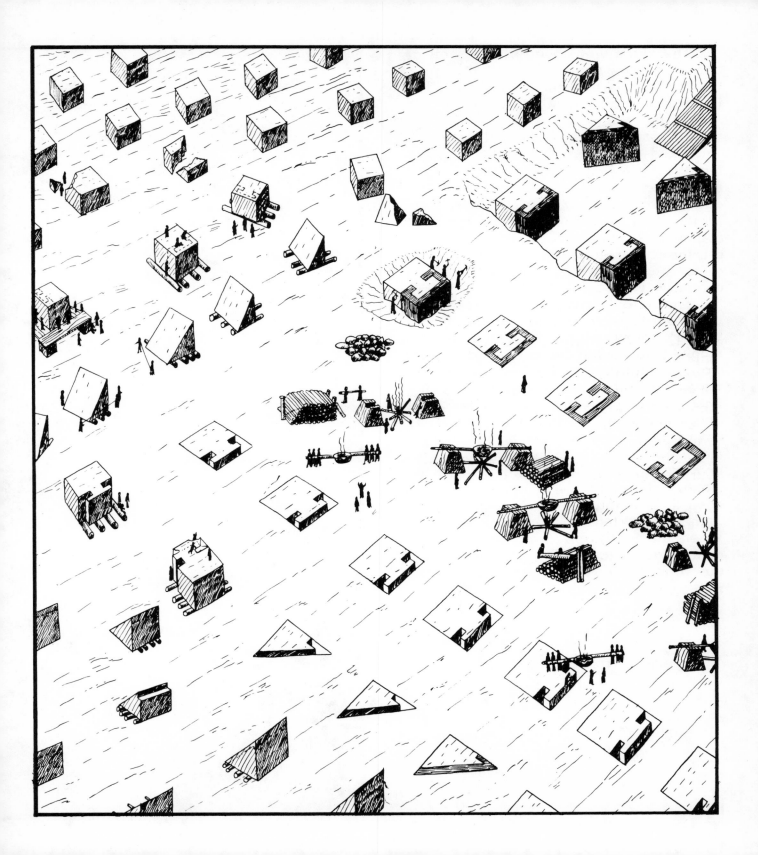

The Atlantans embellished the miles of wall with more than 200 towers. Twenty-eight of them were the city gate towers, 24 at the bridgeheads on the three inner walls and 4 on the long wall. Four water towers stood guard over the canal to the sea, the gateway to Atlantis. Like the walls, the towers were built of varicolored stones and ornamented with metal. The imagination of the Atlantans was such that no two towers were exactly alike.

A TOWER UNDER CONSTRUCTION

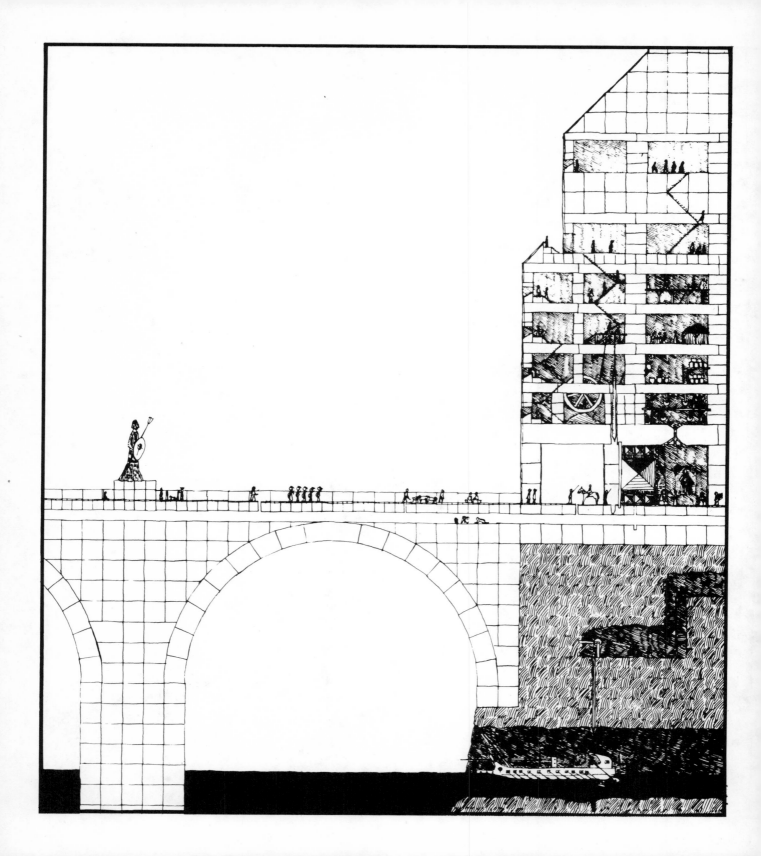

Inside the gate towers were guardrooms, sleeping quarters, stables for horses and elephants, and stores of fodder and ammunition. Horses and chariots patrolled the walls day and night, ready to signal for one or more of the portcullises (there was one at each gate tower) to be lowered if an invader was sighted. (Portcullises below the towers similarly sealed off the subterranean channels.)

The other 200 towers served as substations, lookouts, and communications posts, signaling with flags by day and fires by night.

# Atlantis in Cross Section

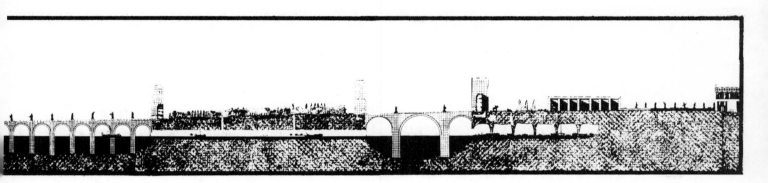

The small scale drawing above shows in cross section the Atlantis Plato described and I have rendered, element by element, in this book; an enlargement is spread across the following ten pages. From the mouth of the canal linking the city with the sea to the Temple of Poseidon standing in the exact center of the Acropolis on the Central Island, here is the capital city of perhaps the greatest empire the world has known.

**Gate Tower in Outer Wall**

**Bridge over Outer Water Belt**

**Canal to Sea**

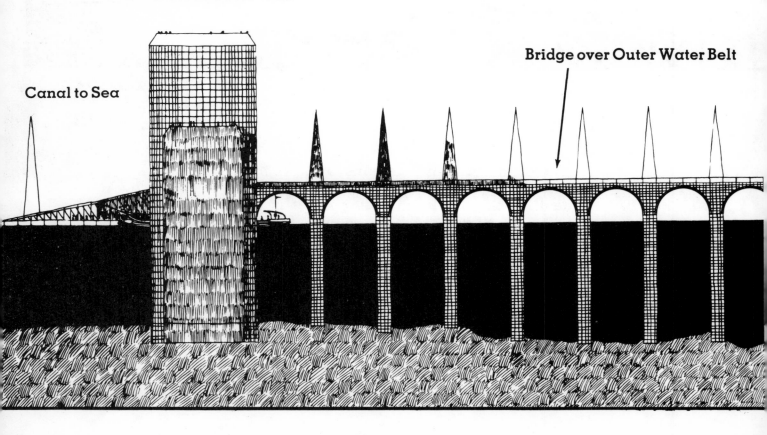

**Bronze Gate Tower in Wall**

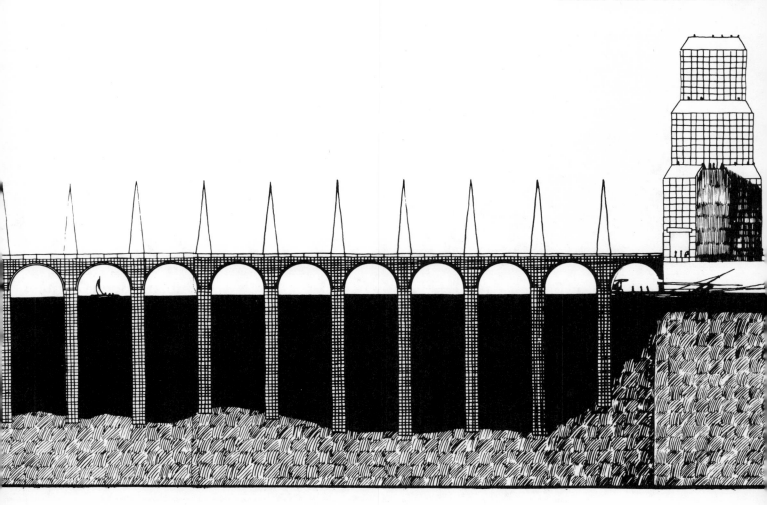

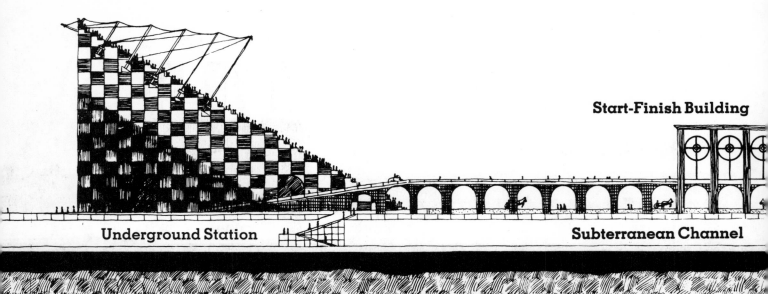

**Grandstand**

**Start-Finish Building**

**Underground Station**

**Subterranean Channel**

**Victors' Temple**

**Bridge over Race Course**

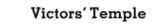

Subterranean Channel

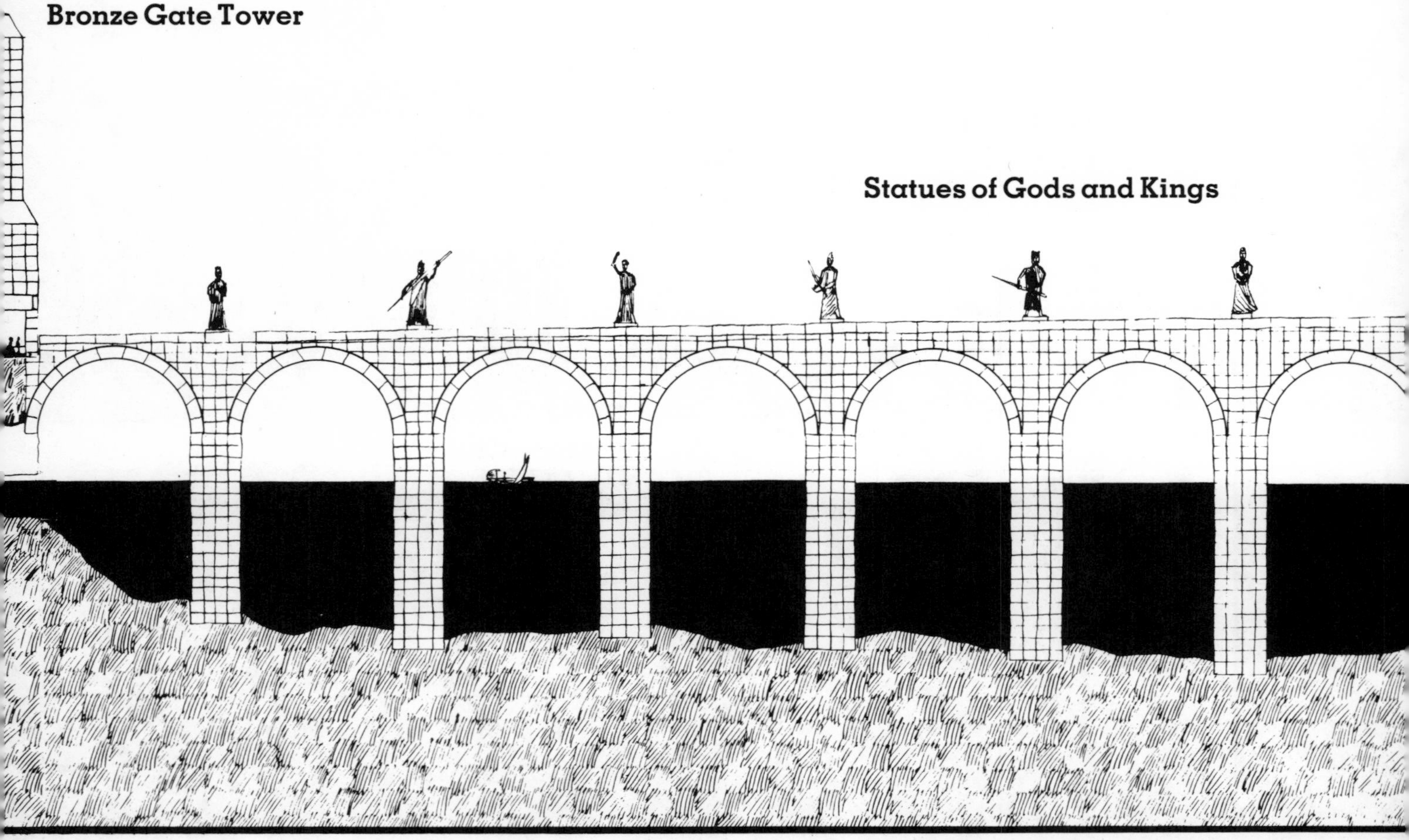

Bronze Gate Tower

Statues of Gods and Kings

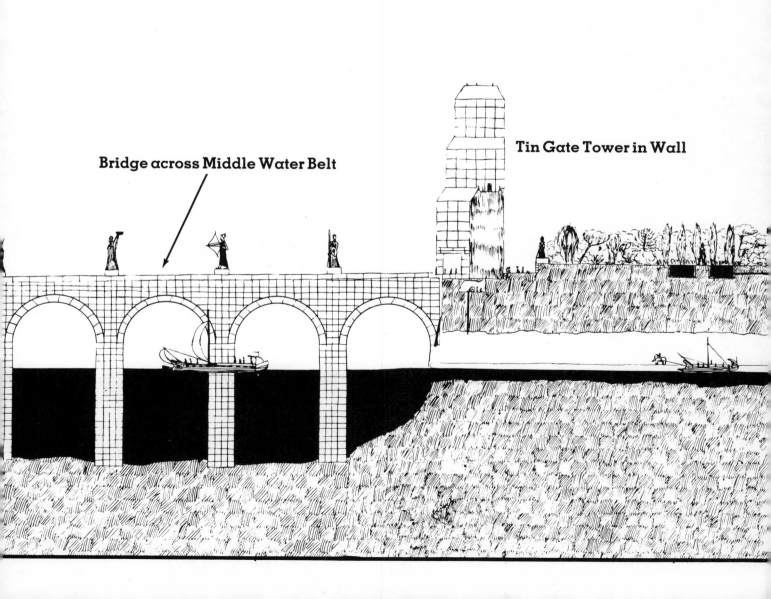

**Bridge across Middle Water Belt**

**Tin Gate Tower in Wall**

Fountains

Tin Gate Tower

Subterranean Channel

Orichalc Gate Tower in Wall

Bridge across Inner Water Belt

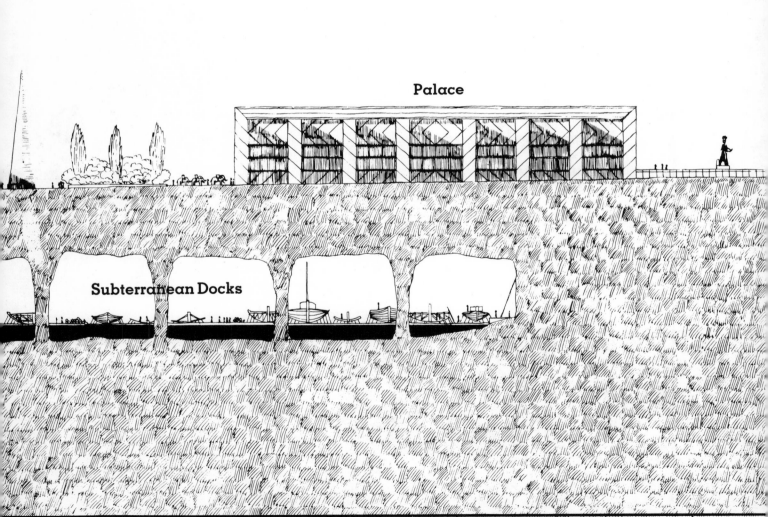

Temple of Poseidon

Colossal Statues in Temple Plaza

ὑστέρῳ δὲ χρόνῳ σεισμῶν ἐξαισίων καὶ κατακλυσμῶν
γενομένων, μιᾶς ἡμέρας καὶ νυκτὸς χαλεπῆς ἐλθούσης,
τό τε παρ᾽ ὑμῶν μάχιμον πᾶν ἀθρόον ἔδυ κατὰ γῆς, ἥ
τε Ἀτλαντὶς νῆσος ὡσαύτως κατὰ τῆς θαλάττης δῦσα
ἠφανίσθη· διὸ καὶ νῦν ἄπορον καὶ ἀδιερεύνητον
γέγονε τὸ ἐκεῖ πέλαγος, πηλοῦ καταβραχέος ἐμποδῶν
ὄντος, ὃν ἡ νῆσος ἱζομένη παρέσχετο.

ΤΙΜΑΙΟΣ

118

# Epilogue

*At a later time there were earthquakes and floods of extraordinary violence, and in a single dreadful day and night all your fighting men were swallowed up by the earth, and the island of Atlantis was similarly swallowed up by the sea and vanished; this is why the sea in that area is to this day impassable to navigation, which is hindered by mud just below the surface, the remains of the sunken island.*

*TIMAEUS*